READABILITY PROGRAM
FOR THE IBM. PC, XT AND AT

SCANDINAVIAN **PC**
SYSTEMS

We wish to thank the following for their contributions:

Roland Larson, Kalmar, program concepts, program development and assistance with documentation
Steven Frankel, Revision of 2nd edition
Elicon Datorteknik AB, Hallstahammar, program development
Mediator Information AB, Växjö, manuscript
Infotext Data Support AB, Växjö, production
Form & Fakta, Ingelstad, graphic design and originals
Kristianstads Boktryckeri AB, Kristianstad, printing and binding

Scandinavian PC Systems
P.O. Box 5004
S-350 05 Växjö
Sweden
Tel. (46)-470-154 00

Scandinavian PC Systems, Inc.
51 Monroe Street, Suite 707A
Rockville, Maryland 20850
USA
Tel. (1)-301-738-8826

Scandinavian PC Systems (UK) Ltd.
P.O. Box 215
Uxbridge UB10 8TG
Tel. (44) 895 679366

ISBN 91-86940-27-9

Preface

Welcome to *Scandinavian PC Systems'* world of inexpensive and simple yet efficient programs. We are firmly convinced that a program should be simple enough and friendly enough to permit you to start working with it after a few minutes, even though you have not worked with any similar programs in the past.

This manual explains how to use your Readability program. It has been written for your PC. For your convenience, the manual is divided into the following chapters.

Why Readability? explains the advantages offered by your Readability program.

Getting started with Readability explains how to make a working copy of your original diskette and also how to install Readability on a disketter or hard-disk system.

Tutorial # 1 – Your first session presents step-by-step instructions that you can follow easily to run through the Readability functions. You'll also have an opportunity to see the different types of result displays provided by Readability.

Here's how Readability operates describes the different options on the main menu, presents the types of files that you can analyze, tells how to eliminate parts of a text in order to obtain more accurate results and explains how to conduct an analysis.

Tutorial # 2 – Understanding readability analysis results describes the different displays created by Readability and explains how to print out the results on your printer.

Basic Readability concepts explains the basic principles of Readability. It also describes what Readability measures and explains how measurements are carried out.

How to improve your writing lists and explains a number factors that you can incorporate into your writing. It also explains the results that appear in the displays and tells what you can do to improve these results.

How Readability was created (written by Roland Larson who designed the program) explains the mathematical basis of the style diagram. This diagram and the measurement methods used in Readability are based on Roland Larson's Readability formula which is an improvement on the Gunning Fog-Index formula.

Appendix A presents the error messages together with their causes, and actions that can be taken to remedy them.

Appendix B presents some useful DOS commands.

Appendix C shows you how you can customize Readability to reflect your own work style.

How to use this manual

To make it easier for you to read and understand this manual, we have used different typefaces as follows:

- Items that you are to type on the keyboard are colored and printed in a different typeface:

  read

- Items that appear on the screen are printed with a different typeface and boxed in as shown below:

```
A>read
```

- Whenever we refer to characters on the keytops of your keyboard, we print either the symbol or the text that appears on the keytop using a different typeface:

  NumLock

You should remember that the menus and other displays presented in this manual are only examples. As a result, they may differ slightly from those that appear on your screen.

Contents

Why Readability?

Readability analyzes your writing on the basis of a sophisticated language philosophy and in-depth knowledge of how language works.

When we speak, the person we are speaking to reacts immediately so that we can see whether what we have said is understood, but this doesn't hold true when we write. Readability tries to give us some idea of how we write by measuring factors that affect readability.

If several thousand people are going to read an article, notice or advertisement you've written and each of them has to spend a minute or so rereading something that's unclear, several days worth of productivity will be lost. You could have avoided this by spending an hour making your writing easier to read. Readability provides valuable assistance to those who wish to write clear, concise texts themselves, and to those who are responsible for improving writing done by others.

If you're already a good writer, Readability can nonetheless provide you with a valuable – and unique – review of your writing.

The more readable your writing is, the easier it will be to get your message across.

HER READABILITY'S AWFUL
—BUT HER STYLE IS GREAT.

Getting started

You will only need to use the information presented in this chapter prior to the first time you use your Readability program. It is important that you follow the instructions step by step.

What you'll need

You'll need an IBM PC, XT or AT with a monochrome monitor (no graphics needed). You can also use an IBM compatible computer. In addition, you'll need at least the following:

- DOS 2.0 or later

- 256 kB RAM memory

- One 360 kB diskette drive

- One unformatted diskette

If you have two diskette drives, a hard disk drive or a color monitor, you will find that your Readability program is even easier to use – and more fun.

Note!
Remember that the examples of menus and other displays shown in this manual may differ slightly from those that appear on your screen.

If you have two diskette drives

If your computer has a hard disk drive, go directly to the section entitled *If you have a hard disk drive*.

- Insert your DOS diskette in drive A and close the latch. (Hereafter, we assume that you'll close the latch each time you insert a diskette.)

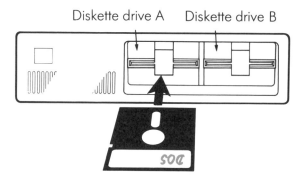

- Switch on power to the computer.

When the system prompt (A>) appears on the screen, you may continue. (If you have to enter the date and time, follow the instructions in the User's Manual that accompanies your computer.)

Copying your original diskette

You should never use the diskette that accompanies this manual to work with. The very first thing you should do is make a backup copy according to the following instructions:

Note!
You can make as many copies as you wish, but only for your own use.

- Type the following on the keyboard:

  ```
  format b:/s
  ```

- Press the ↵ key.

The computer will now prepare (format) the unformatted diskette so that information can be stored on it. The following will appear on the screen:

```
A>format b:/s
Insert new diskette for drive B:
and strike any key when ready
```

- Insert the unformatted diskette in diskette drive B.
- Press the ↵ key.

When formatting is completed, a message such as the following will appear on the screen:

```
A>format b:/s
Insert new diskette for drive B:
and strike any key when ready

Formatting . . . Format complete

System transferred
   362496 bytes total disk space
    40960 bytes used by system
   321536 bytes available on disk

Format another (Y/N)?
```

- Press the **N** key to conclude formatting.

The system prompt will then appear on the screen again:

```
A>_
```

- Remove the DOS diskette from diskette drive A.
- Insert the original diskette into diskette drive A.
- Type the following on the keyboard:

  system

- Press the ↵ key.

The computer now starts to copy the content of the original diskette onto the diskette in drive B. The following will appear on the screen when copying is completed:

```
*********** Copying the program files ***********

This will take a few minutes. Please wait..

Copying is completed!
A>_
```

- Remove the original diskette from diskette drive A.
- Insert the DOS diskette into diskette drive A.
- Type the following:

  b: doscopy

- Press the ⏎ key.

The computer now starts to copy part of the content of the DOS diskette onto the diskette in drive B. This will make it unnecessary for you, in the future, to insert the DOS diskette before starting up your Readability program.

Note!
If the words File not found *appear on the screen during copying, everything may still be OK. This occurs sometimes on personal computers not made by IBM.*

The following will appear on the screen when copying is completed:

```
*********** Copying the DOS files ***********

This will take a few minutes. Please wait...

Copying is completed!
A>_
```

- Remove the DOS diskette from diskette drive A.

- Remove your working diskette (hereinafter called the program diskette) from diskette drive B.

- Label the program diskette.

When you have made your copy (the program diskette) of the original diskette, put the original away in some safe place. Henceforth, you should use the program diskette every time you work with your Readability program.

If you have a hard disk drive

You should never use your original Readability diskette to work with. Instead, you should immediately copy its content onto the hard disk. Proceed as follows:

- Turn on the power to your computer.

When the system prompt (C>) appears on the screen you may continue. (If you have to enter the date and time, follow the instructions in the User's Manual that accompanies your computer.)

- Insert your original diskette into diskette drive A.

Diskette drive A

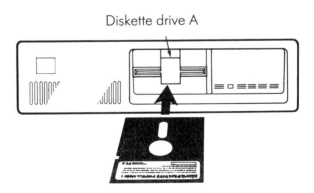

- Type the following:

  a: hdcopy

- Press the ← key.

The computer copies the content of your original diskette onto the hard disk. Consequently, you will not need your original diskette in the future when you wish to use Readability.

When copying is completed, the following appears on the screen:

```
*********** Copying the program files ***********

This will take a few minutes. Please wait...

Copying is completed!
C>_
```

- Remove the original diskette from diskette drive A.

Now that you have made a copy of your original diskette, you should keep the original in a safe place.

Note!
HDCOPY.BAT creates a subdirectory called SPCSREAD. This occurs during installation and all files are copied into this subdirectory.

Copying Readability onto other diskettes

If you want a copy of Readability on another diskette, proceed as follows:

- Check that the system prompt (A> or C>) appears on the screen.

- Insert your program diskette (Readability) in diskette drive A.

Insert the target diskette onto which you wish to copy Readability in diskette drive B.

- Type:

  a: install

- Press the ↵ key.

When copying is completed, the following will appear on the screen:

```
Copying is completed!

A>_
```

Readability has now been copied onto the diskette in drive B.

HOW CAN SO MANY WRITE
SO MUCH THAT IS
GRASPED BY SO FEW?

Tutorial # 1 – Your first session

If you have made a backup copy of your original diskette or installed the program on your hard disk, you can proceed with your first Readability session. This chapter presents instructions on how to conduct a simple analysis of a text and examine the results.

If you are using diskette drives, remember that you must work with your program diskette and not with the original diskette.

Preparations

● Start the computer.

If you only have diskette drives:

● Insert the Readability diskette in diskette drive A.

● Hold down **Ctrl** and **Alt** and tap **Del**.

You can also start your Readability program as follows when the system prompt (A>) appears on the screen.

● Type:

  read

● Press the ↵ key.

If you have a hard disk:

● When the system prompt (C>) appears, type:

  read

● Press the ↵ key.

When the program has been loaded, the following will appear:

```
                    Scandinavian PC Systems
                    presents Readability

               for the IBM PC, XT and AT 1.0

                    Serial No. *******

  1.  How your Readability program works.
  2.  Analyze a text.
  3.  Examine results of previous analysis.
  9.  Select background color.
  0.  Exit from Readability program.

               Select an option:

     Copyright (C) 1983, 1987 by Roland Larson
     Copyright (C) 1987 by Scandinavian PC Systems and
     Elicon Datorteknik AB
```

Backing out with F1

In your Readability program, you can always try out something to see what will happen. This makes it easier to explore the function keys and menus. If something unexpected happens, you can always back out of the situation very easily by pressing **F1**. This will take you back where you were without any changes having been made. If you press **F1** repeatedly, you will be returned to the main menu.

If you need help

Your Readability program has a built-in help function (**F10**) that provides you with brief, helpful information while you are working. It can be used any time, except when the main menu screen is being displayed.

Analyzing a text

Note!
Remember that the screen display examples shown in this manual may differ somewhat from those that appear on your screen. The examples in the manual are for a diskette-drive system. If you have a hard disk, you may see C:\SPCSREAD\ instead of A:

Selecting an option from the main menu

The following should now appear on your screen. If it doesn't, you must return to the section headed ***Preparations***.

```
                    Scandinavian PC Systems
                     presents Readability

                 for the IBM PC, XT and AT 1.0

                    Serial No. *******


  1.   How your Readability program works.
  2.   Analyze a text.
  3.   Examine results of previous analysis.
  9.   Select background color.
  0.   Exit from Readability program.

                 Select an option:

       Copyright (C) 1983, 1987 by Roland Larson
       Copyright (C) 1987 by Scandinavian PC Systems and
       Elicon Datorteknik AB
```

You will now analyze a text that is already present on your program diskette.

- Press **F2**.

Selecting a text

The following now appears on the screen:

```
Text analysis using Readability

A:\EXAMPLE.TXT

Specify filename:

1M-menu  2  3Dspls  4Files  5Files*  6  7  8  9  10Help
```

You can select the text you wish to analyze by moving the highlight onto the name of the text by means of the arrow keys. Then press the ↵ key.

You will now select a text to analyze. Since EXAMPLE.TXT is already highlighted, you can select it by:

● Pressing the ↵ key.

The following now appears at the bottom of the screen:

```
Specify where the result is to be stored (A:\)

>_
```

You must now tell the program where you want the analysis results to be stored. The program proposes a storage location which, in this case, is the diskette in drive A (drive C if you have a hard disk). Here, you will accept the program's proposal by:

● Pressing the ↵ key.

The following now appears at the bottom of the screen:

```
Text title:
```

Here, you can specify a descriptive title for the text that you are going to analyze. For example, you may want to use the author's name or a brief summary of the text's contents.

● Type:

My first example

● Press the ↵ key.

The following now appears on the screen:

```
                    Text analysis using Readability

  A:\EXAMPLE.TXT

         Sentences that fall outside the teardrop outline for
         the selected analysis pattern you select will be
         saved and used later when you
         examine the results.

              1.   Ideal area
              2.   Young people's book
              3.   Newspaper article
              4.   Advertising copy
              5.   Novel
              6.   Magazine feature story
              7.   Technical manuals
              8.   Government report
              9.   Bureaucratic gobbledygook

  Specify analysis pattern (1):

  Esc = Exit
```

A sentence that falls outside the teardrop outline is considered deviant, and it is saved by the program in a special result file named EXAMPLE.DEV.

If none of patterns 2–9 are suitable for your text, you should probably select pattern 1 (the normal diagram). Note that patterns 7, 8 and 9 are not to be considered good examples. They are included simply to show how technical manuals, government reports and bureaucratic memorandums are usually written. We hope that your writing will be better than typical examples of these. When the analysis is complete, you can examine the sentences that were found to be outside the selected feardrop outline (deviant sentences).

Since the text in the example is general in nature, you will select pattern 1 (normal diagram). Since the program uses this as the default, all you have to do to select pattern 1 is to press the ↵ key (you do not have to type in 1).

Proceed as follows to select pattern 1:

● Press the ↵ key.

Preliminary checks

Before the program starts to analyze the text, you are given an opportunity to make certain that everything is the way you want it. Your selections are presented on the screen as follows:

```
              Text analysis using Readability

A:\EXAMPLE.TXT

Result:             A:\EXAMPLE
Text title:         My first example
Analysis pattern:   1 Normal diagram

Press ↵ if everything is OK. Otherwise, press Esc.


Esc = Exit
```

If you have made a mistake or change your mind, you can start again from the beginning:

- Press **Esc**.

- Return to the section headed *Selecting an option from the main menu*.

If everything is OK:

- Press the ↵ key.

Starting the analysis

The program now reads and analyzes the text. While this is in progress, the style diagram appears on the screen and the program enters a dot as each sentence is analyzed. When the program has read and analyzed the entire text, the results are stored on disk (diskette or hard disk) under filename EXAMPLE.FX.

Style diagram for the text

The following appears on the screen when analysis is finished:

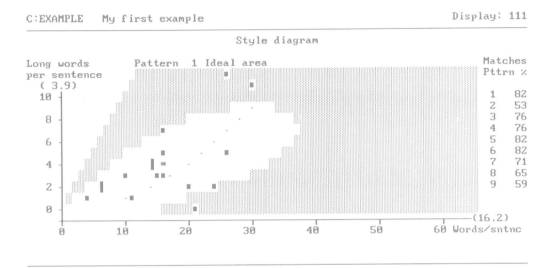

The percentages of sentences that lie within the different teardrop outlines appear at right. Analysis pattern 1 is highlighted. As you see, 83 % of the sentences are within the teardrop outline used for analysis pattern 1. By checking to see which percentage is largest, you can see which of the patterns (2–9) your text resembles most. By pressing F8, you can see what the different patterns are called. Later, we'll see, each sentence will be labelled based on where it's located in the diagram.

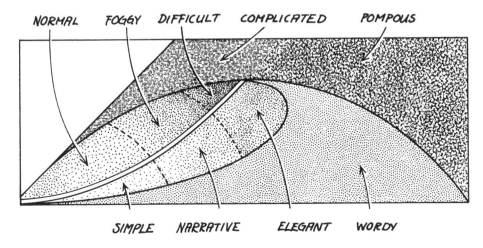

Printing deviant sentences

If you have a printer, you can print out a list of all of the deviant sentences. The program presents you with the first few words in each deviant sentence and tells you the line on which the sentence is located.

Proceed as follows to print a list of the deviant sentences on the printer:

- Make certain that the printer is ON-LINE (ready for printing).

- Press **F7**.

- Press **F1**.

A list of the deviant sentences will now be printed.

You can now continue by examining another result display.

Selecting other result displays

There are 15 displays in addition to the style diagram (which you have already seen).

Proceed as follows to obtain a list of the other displays that are available:

- Press **F4**.

The following appears:

```
C:EXAMPLE   My first example                              Display: 111

         ┌─────────────────────────────────────────────────────────────────┐
         │ * Select one of 16 result displays. Specify number and press ↵    │
Long w   │─────────────────────────────────────────────────────────────────│hes
per se   │ SENTENCE ANALYSIS                  SENTENCE PROFILE               │n %
  ( 3.   │ ────────────────────────────      ────────────────────────────   │
   10    │  11  Style diagram                 31  Types of sentences         │ 82
         │  111-119 Analysis patterns 1-9     32  Long words per sentence    │ 53
    8    │  12  Types of sentences            33  Sentence lengths           │ 76
         │  13  Long words per sentence                                      │ 76
    6    │  14  Sentence lengths              SUMMARIES                      │ 82
         │  15  Consecutive short words       ────────────────────────────  │ 82
    4    │  16  Consecutive long words        41  Overall evaluation         │ 71
         │                                    42  General comments           │ 65
    2    │ WORD ANALYSIS                       43  Number of sentences and words│ 59
         │ ────────────────────────────                                     │
    0    │  21  Word lengths                                                 │
         │  22  Bricks                                                       │
    0    │  23  Mortar and bricks                                            │nc
         │  24  Comments on word selection                                   │
         └─────────────────────────────────────────────────────────────────┘

Specify display number:
```

You can select the result display that you wish to observe by typing in its number and then pressing the ↵ key.

Looking at the general evaluation

You can, of course, look at the displays in any desired sequence. In this example you will first look at display 41 which presents a general evaluation.

To select display 41, respond to the following prompt as set forth below:

Specify display number:

- Type:

  41

- Press the ↵ key.

This display presents a general evaluation of six factors. Here, you can read the final value assigned to the text for each factor. Don't worry right now about what all six factors measure, that will be covered in Tutorial # 2. For now, note that the distance from the focal point to the ideal curve is 1.3.

Focal Point

A text's focal point is the point on the diagram that represents the average sentence length and the average number of long words per sentence. (All words containing seven or more characters are defined as long by Readability.)

Useful tips

Readability provides you with tips and comments on each display. You can learn a lot by reading these. Right now, you'll take a look at the tips provided for the general evaluation of the text used in this example.

Proceed as follows:

- Press **F8**.

Here, you can compare the different values obtained for the text with those presented in the tips. For example, you can see that the Readability Index is 40 (good). The sentences shown on the style diagram have a spread of 8.6. This is also good.

Ideal diagram display

Readability also presents an ideal diagram for each display. You can compare the diagrams obtained for the text used in this example with the ideal diagrams. You will now take a look at the ideal diagram for display 41.

- Press **F9**.

Before you select the next display, you will take a look at the available displays. This list contains the names of the different result displays. However, you can select the desired display directly by typing in its number.

- Press **F4**.

Looking at the general comments

You will now look at display 42 to see the general comments.

- Type:

  42

- Press the ← key.

Here, you see some advice that can help you improve your writing. When you have finished reading this advice, you can look at another display.

Looking at the numbers of sentences and words

- Press **F4**.

- Type:

  43

- Press the ← key.

Display 43 presents the numbers of sentences and words in the entire text.

Now let's look at display 12 which presents the types of sentences.

Looking at the types of sentences

- Press **F4**.
- Type:

  12

- Press the ↵ key.

Each sentence in the text is classified as one of the following types, based upon the number of words in the sentence, and the proportion of those words which are considered long because they contain more than six letters:

- **Simple** – a short sentence made up almost entirely of short words

- **Normal** – a short sentence containing a few long words

- **Narrative** – a medium length sentence containing a few long words

- **Foggy** – a medium length sentence with several long words

- **Elegant** – a fairly long sentence with several long words

- **Difficult** – a fairly long sentence with a lot of long words

- **Complicated** – a fairly long sentence with too many long words to be easily understood

- **Pompous** – a sentence with too many words to be easily understood, and which usually has too many long words as well

- **Wordy** – a sentence with too many words to be easily understood, but which has relatively few long words.

Sentences labelled complicated, pompous or wordy fall outside the teardrop that indicates good writing. You may want to change them to improve your text's readability.

Looking at the ideal diagram display

Proceed as follows to look at the ideal diagram display:

- Press **F9**.

Looking at word lengths

- Type:

  21

- Press the ↵ key.

Display 21 presents the word lengths. Here, you see that the average word length is 4.7 letters. 20 % of all words in our example have only 1, 2 or 3 letters. Does 20 % seem right to you? Let's check by taking a look at the ideal diagram display.

- Press **F9**.

The diagram shows that 20 % is OK! The diagram also shows that having many short words is highly desirable. Let's take a look at Readability's tips.

- Press **F8**.

Read what appears on the screen.

You can call up a list of all words having a specified number (or more) letters. Let's look at all words that have 13 or more letters (for example). Proceed as follows:

- Type:

  13-

- Press the ↵ key.

The following now appears:

```
                        Word lengths

1   AUTOMATICALLY
1   SOPHISTICATED

13-      1 brick(s)
```

You are shown the words that have 13 or more letters and the program indicates how many times they occurred in the text. Both occurred once. Bricks will be explained later.

Looking at long-word runs

The term "run", as used here, refers to one or more consecutive words. You will now look at display 16 which presents the long-word runs. Your Readability program saves runs of three or more long words. A word is considered long if it has seven or more characters. "Distant" is thus a long word.

Since you know that you wish to look at display 16, you don't have to call up the list of displays. Instead, you can type in the display number directly.

• Type:

  16

• Press the ↵ key.

The long-word runs now appear. The display shows that 29 % of the runs consist of only one long word. 16 % of the runs contain two long words. 3 % of the runs consist of three long words. 1 % of the runs consist of four long words.

Take a look at the ideal diagram display:

• Press **F9**.

Now take a look at the tips:

• Press **F8**.

You will now call up all of the long-word runs consisting of four or more words. Proceed as follows:

• Type:

  4 –

• Press the ↵ key.

The following now appears further down on the screen:

```
Processing program advances automatically
------------------------------------------------------
Page 1    Line No.: 21    Consecutive long words: 3      Press ←┘
```

You are shown the only long-word run containing four or more words and told where you will find it in the text, namely on line 21.

- Press the ←┘ key.

Printing long-word runs on the printer

If you have a printer, you can print out all of the long-word runs containing three or more long words. The printout presents all of the words in each run and indicates where (line number) in the text each run can be found.

Proceed as follows to print out the long-word runs on the printer:

- Check that the printer is ON-LINE (ready for printing).
- Press **F7**.
- Press **F2**.

Mortar and bricks

The last display that you are going to look at in this example is display 23. It presents the percentages of mortar and bricks in the text. The term "mortar" as used here refers to the 450 most frequently used words in the English language. The term "bricks" refers to non-mortar words used to convey information.

Proceed as follows to select display 23:

- Type:

  23

- Press the ←┘ key.

The bar at right indicates the percentage of bricks in the text.

Normal text contains approximately 40 % bricks. A higher value indicates that the text is more difficult than a normal text. The text used in this example has 34 % bricks. The remaining 66 % is mortar (words included in the 450 most frequently used words in the English language).

Exiting from Readability

In this example, you have looked at several of the Readability displays. In the chapter entitled *Understanding readability analysis results*, you will find descriptions of all of the result displays.

You will now exit from the Readability program.

First, you must return to the main menu:

• Press **F1**.

The main menu appears. To exit from Readability, you select Exit on the main menu:

• Press **0**.

• Press the ↵ key.

When the system prompt (A>) appears, you can remove your diskette, thus concluding the Readability session.

READABILITY TELLS ME MY
FOCAL POINT'S TOO HIGH – BUT
I'M BUILT LIKE A MILK BOTTLE.

Here's how Readability operates

We shall now assume that your Readability program has been installed as set forth in the chapter entitled *Getting started*, and loaded as explained in "Your first session".

When the program has been loaded, the following appears:

```
                    Scandinavian PC Systems
                      presents Readability

                   for the IBM PC, XT and AT 1.0

                      Serial No. *******

 1.   How your Readability program works.
 2.   Analyze a text.
 3.   Examine results of previous analysis.
 9.   Select background color.
 0.   Exit from Readability program.

                    Select an option:

       Copyright (C) 1983, 1987 by Roland Larson
       Copyright (C) 1987 by Scandinavian PC Systems and
       Elicon Datorteknik AB
```

Brief review of main menu

You can select options from the main menu in two ways:

- Type the desired number (1, 2, 3, 9 or 0).

- Press the ↵ key.

However, you can speed things up a little by using the function keys:

- Press the desired function key (**F1**, **F2**, **F3**, **F9** or **F10**).

Note!
Function key **F10** *corresponds to selection 0 on the menu.*

Option 1 – How your Readability program works

When the main menu appears on the screen:

- Press **F1**.

Information about the following now appears:

- The files that you can analyze.

- How you can eliminate parts of a text to improve analysis.

Both of the above are discussed in greater detail in the next chapter.

- Press any key to return to the main menu.

Option 2 – Analyze a text

When you select option 2 (Analyze a text), you must type the following:

- Where the program can find the text (disk drive, subdirectory).

- The name of the text (filename).

- Where the results are to be stored.

- Which analysis pattern you wish to have the text compared with.

In addition, you can type:

- A title so that you can easily identify the text when you look at the results later.

You can look at a list of all the files that can be analyzed or a list of the files that have been previously analyzed.

You can also look at texts located on other disks (hard disk or diskettes in other drives).

This function is explained in greater detail in the sector entitled *Which files can you analyze?*

Option 3 – Examine results of previous analyses

When you select option 3, a list appears on the screen. This list contains the names of the results of previous analyses.

You can also look at texts located on other disks (hard disk or diskettes in other drives).

This function is explained in greater detail in the the section entitled *Which files can you analyze?*.

Option 9 – Select background color

If you have a color monitor, you can choose between two color combinations:

- Black background with yellow and green text.
- Blue background with yellow and green text.
- Pressing F9 toggles you between the two color combinations.

If you have a single-color monitor, nothing happens when you press **F9**.

Option 0 – Exit from Readability program

- Press **F10** to exit from Readability.

Useful tips on printing

If a printer is connected to your computer you can, at any time, obtain a paper copy of the screen content.

Proceed as follows:

- Check that the printer is ON-LINE (ready for printing).
- Hold down the ⇧ key and tap **PrtSc**.

The screen content will be copied over onto the printer. On some printers, certain special characters and boxes may not be printed out exactly as they appear on the screen since all printers do not support all of the graphics characters that are used. However, the text should be the same as it appeared on the screen.

Which files can you analyze?

Texts that you can analyze must:

● Have been written using the Scandinavian PC Systems word processing program or another one which writes in an ASCII format.

Or

● Have been written using some other word processing program and then saved as or converted to ASCII files.

Converting a file to ASCII

When you save a text in ASCII format, all or most of the special characters are eliminated. These can include the markings used for headings, bolding and underlining. The specific special characters that are eliminated will depend on which word processing program you were using.

Most word processing programs include a program called "Convert" or something similar. This program can be used to automatically eliminate the special characters that would otherwise disturb the Readability analysis. The converted file is called an ASCII file, although the word processing program in question may call it "DOS text", "plain text", "output file" or something similar.

Remember that if you convert a text file to ASCII format, you should also save it in its original form. This can be done using the "Save" function in your word processing program or by first copying the file and then converting the copy. You should keep a copy of the original since when you convert to ASCII, you will loose most of or all of the special codes (format codes) that have been entered into the text. Consequently, you would have to do a lot of work before using it again with your word processing program.

You can use DOS command TYPE to see whether or not a file has become an ASCII file and – even more importantly – to print out a copy of the file you'll be analyzing so that you can easily refer to it. To print the text file named EXAMPLE.ASC (supplied with Readability):

- Be sure your printer is ON-LINE (ready for printing)
- Type

  `type example.asc`

- Hold down the **CTRL** key and press **P**
- Press the ⏎ key

The text file named EXAMPLE.ASC will then be printed. When the printer stops:

- Hold down the **CTRL** key and press **P** again.

How to eliminate parts of a text

It is not necessary to analyze an entire text. You can eliminate part of the text or different parts of the text. You do this by marking the parts of the text that are to be analyzed by means of special characters before starting analysis.

If you do not wish to eliminate one or more parts of your text, you can now proceed to the section headed *Starting analysis*. If you do wish to eliminate one or more parts of your text, you should work with a copy of the text and not with the original.

If Readability has been loaded into your computer, the first thing to do is exit from the Readability program. To do this, proceed as follows:

- Press **F1**, whereupon the main menu will appear.
- Press **F10** to exit from Readability.

Start your word processing program and load (retrieve) the ASCII file that you have created.

- Move the cursor to the location immediately preceding the text you wish to eliminate.

- Hold down the **Alt** key and enter the following on the numeric keypad (located at right on most keyboards):

  244

- Release the **Alt** key.

You have now marked the beginning of the part of the text that is not to be analyzed with character "ſ".

The end of the part of the text that is not to be analyzed must also be marked, but using a different character, namely "ﾍ".

- Move the cursor to the location immediately after the part of the text that is not to be analyzed.

- Hold down the **Alt** key and type the following on the numeric keypad at right:

  245

- Release the **Alt** key.

You can use the same procedure again if you wish to eliminate additional parts of the text before starting the analysis.

Readability and headings

You should always eliminate headings so that your analysis will be accurate. If you do not do so, each heading is chained to the sentence that follows immediately after it.

This is because Readability defines the end of a sentence as follows:

- Period followed by an upper case letter.
- Colon followed by an upper case letter.
- Question mark followed by an upper case letter.
- Explanation point followed by an upper case letter.
- Semicolon.

Since a period does not normally follow a heading, the heading is chained to the next sentence, and this usually creates a sentence that is extra long. However, if you put a period after the heading, the heading itself will be considered a sentence.

Starting analysis

We shall now set forth the steps you should take before starting analysis.

Selecting the text

When the main menu appears on the screen:

- Press **F2**.

The following now appears:

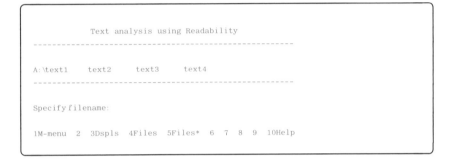

```
          Text analysis using Readability
    ------------------------------------------------------

A:\text1    text2      text3      text4
    ------------------------------------------------------

Specify filename:

1M-menu  2  3Dspls  4Files  5Files*  6  7  8  9  10Help
```

The names of the files that can be analyzed and are present on your program diskette appear on the screen. If you have a hard disk, the files present in the same subdirectory as the Readability program are shown. Files having the following filename extensions are not shown on the screen since these files do not normally contain texts.

.BAK

.BAS

.COM

.EXE

.FX

.FY

.FZ

.RDB

.SYS

Files extended with .FX, .FY and .FZ are created by the Readability program when it analyzes a text.

If the text you are going to analyze is among those whose names are shown on the screen, proceed as follows:

● Use the arrow keys to highlight the desired text.

● Press the ↵ key.

If the desired text is not included among those shown on the screen, you must tell the program where to find it. To do this, you must respond to the following prompt:

```
Specify filename:_
```

If the desired text is on some other diskette, insert the diskette in drive B.

● Type:

  b:

● Press the ↵ key.

A new list of texts that can be analyzed appears. However, your text may be present in a subdirectory. In such case, you must specify for the program the path leading to the text. If, for example, your text is in a subdirectory named WORD, you should proceed as follows:

● Type:

  \word\

● Press the ↵ key.

A list of the files that can be processed by Readability that are present in the subdirectory named WORD now appears.

However, if you know the name of your text and you know exactly where it is located, you can enter the drive, the subdirectory (if any) and the filename directly.

Example:

- Type:

  c:\word\text1

Specifying where to store the analysis results

After you have specified which text you are going to analyze, you must tell the program where to store the analysis results. The following prompt appears:

```
Specify where to store the results (A:\)
>_
```

Here, the program proposes that you store your results on the diskette in drive A. If you accept the proposal:

- Press the ↵ key.

However, you can also select some other drive or subdirectory. If, for example, you wish to store your results on the diskette in drive A in a subdirectory named SPCREAD:

- Type:

  a:\spcsread\

- Press the ↵ key.

Note that if you wish to store your results in a subdirectory, the subdirectory must have been previously established.

If you have analyzed the same text previously, the following appears:

```
Results:    b:\text1 already exists.

Do you wish to overwrite it (Y/N)?
```

If you have no reason to preserve the previous results, you can write over them.

• Type:

    y

If you wish to preserve the previous results, you must enter another filename for the new results.

• Type:

    n

The program now prompts you as follows:

```
Specify desired filename for results:_
```

Type in the new filename:

• Type:

    newres   (for example)

• Press the ↵ key.

Specifying a title for the results

The following now appears on the screen:

```
Title of results:
```

Here, you can enter the title that you wish to give to the results. You might enter the author's name or enter a sentence that describes the text in question. Whatever you enter will appear on the screen as a reference later on when you look at the results. You are permitted to enter a maximum of 52 characters.

• Type the desired title.

• Press the ↵ key.

Selecting an analysis pattern

The following now appears on the screen:

```
                    Text analysis using Readability

A:\filenamn

        ┌─────────────────────────────────────────────────────┐
        │         Sentences that fall outside the teardrop outline │
        │         are saved and used later when you                │
        │         examine the results.                             │
        └─────────────────────────────────────────────────────┘

        1.   Normal diagram
        2.   Young people's book
        3.   Newspaper article
        4.   Advertising copy
        5.   Novel
        6.   Magazine feature story
        7.   Technical manual
        8.   Government report
        9.   Bureaucratic gobbledygook

        Specify analysis pattern (1):

Esc = Exit
```

Here, you select the analysis pattern with which you wish to compare your text. Sentences that fall within the teardrop outline are considered normal by your Readability program. Any sentence that lies outside the teardrop outline is considered deviant, and it is saved by the program in a special result file named EXAMPLE.FY.

After analysis is completed, you will be able to look at the sentences that deviate from the teardrop outline.

If you wish to use pattern 1 (normal diagram):

• Press the ⏎ key.

If you wish to use any of patterns 2–9:

• Type the pattern number:

  2   (for example):

• Press the ⏎ key.

Checking your selections and starting analysis

Finally, you are given an opportunity to check the selections you have made. If you have made a mistake, or if you change your mind, you can start again from the beginning:

• Press the **Esc** key.

If everything is OK:

• Press the ↵ key.

Observing analysis

The program now analyzes the text and saves the results on disk. As this proceeds, you can watch the style diagram being plotted on the screen. Each sentence is indicated by a dot. The next chapter explains how to interpret this diagram.

Tutorial # 2 – Understanding readability analysis results

This chapter explains the displays created in a Readability analysis. Here, you will learn how to call up the different displays and compare your values with the ideal values.

Selecting an analysis result

If you read this section immediately after you have analyzed a text, the text's style diagram will be shown on your screen. If all you wish to look at is this particular result, you can skip the rest of this section and proceed with the section headed *Brief submenu description*.

To select a particular analysis result, you must first start the Readability program if it is not already running.

When the main menu appears:

- Press **F3**.

If the main menu is not shown, but if the submenu at the bottom of the screen includes 3Dspls or 3Load:

- Press **F3**.

The computer presents a list of the results that are available. This list is created from the default drive and subdirectory (if any).

If the result you wish to work with is included on the list:

- Highlight the desired result using the arrow keys.
- Press the ←┘ key.

If the result you wish to work with is not present on the list, you must tell the program where to find it. The following prompt appears:

```
Specify filename:_
```

If the text is on another diskette, insert it in one of the diskette drives (drive B, for example).

● Type:

   b:

● Press the ↵ key.

A new display showing the Readability results that are available appears.

Your file may also be present in a subdirectory. In such case, you must specify a path so that the computer can find it. If, for example, your file is in a subdirectory called WORD:

● Type:

   \word\

● Press the ↵ key.

A new display showing the texts present in the subdirectory called WORD appears.

If you know the name of your text and its location, you can enter the drive, subdirectory (if any) and the filename directly. Let's assume, for example, that the Readability results for a text named TEXT1 are located on the hard disk in a subdirectory named WORD:

● Type:

   c:\word\text1

● Press the ↵ key.

When you have selected the particular result that you wish to look at, the text's style diagram appears on the screen. Here's a typical style diagram:

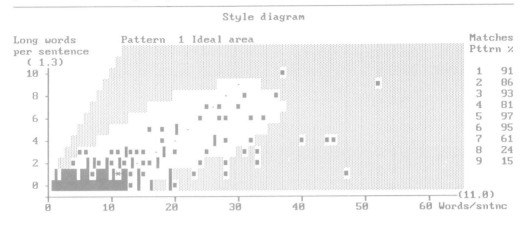

Remember that you can have a copy of the screen content printed out at any time if a printer is connected to your computer. To obtain a paper copy of the screen content, proceed as follows:

- Make certain that the printer is ON-LINE (ready for printing).

- Hold down the ⇧ key and tap **PrtSc**.

Brief submenu description

The Readability program creates results that enable you to study a number of analysis displays that can tell you a great deal about your writing. Before proceeding to look at the displays, it might be advisable to quickly review the options available to you on the submenu that appears at the bottom of your screen:

```
1M-menu   2Analys   3Load   4Cntent   5Plot   6Sntnc   7Print   8Tips 9Ideal   10Help
```

To invoke a function on the submenu, you simply press the corresponding function key. To select 3Load, you press **F3**, etc. The submenu functions shown are available at any time while the submenu appears on the screen. 5Plot and 6Sntnc only appear when you are looking at the text's style diagram.

1M-menu

This function permits you to exit at any time from the result display that is currently shown and return to the main menu.

• Press **F1**.

2Analys

Permits you to leave the currently shown result display at any time and analyze a new text.

• Press **F2**.

3Load

Permits you to leave the currently shown result display at any time and retrieve (load) a new Readability result display.

• Press **F3**.

4Content

Enables you to call up at any time a display showing a list of all of the result displays that are available.

• Press **F4**.

5Plot

When the style diagram appears on the screen, each individual sentence is represented by a dot on the diagram. When more than one sentence is plotted at the same location on the drawing, the dot grows larger for each sentence that is added. These dots can be replaced with numbers that indicate how many sentences have been plotted at each position.

• Press **F5**.

Pressing **F5** toggles between numbers and dots. The highest number that can appear is a 9. This means that a 9 will appear even though more than nine sentences have been plotted at the position in question.

6Sntnc

• Press **F6**.

Sentences that fall outside the teardrop outline that you selected are considered by the program as deviant. Using the arrow keys, you can move the cursor around in the style diagram to mark deviant sentences. Proceed as follows to mark a deviant sentence.

• Press the ↵ key.

If there is more than one deviant sentence at a single position, you can press the ↵ key repeatedly to see all of the sentences.

7Print

• Press **F7**.

When you select this function, the following submenu appears at the bottom of the screen:

```
F1=Print deviant sentences  F2=Print long-word runs F10=Help   Esc=exit
```

This gives you an opportunity to print out the first words in each deviant sentence together with its page number and line number.

Proceed as follows to print out a list of the deviant sentences:

• Check that the printer is ON-LINE (ready for printing).

• Press **F1**.

When printing is finished, you can leave this submenu:

• Press **Esc**.

You can also print out a list of all long-word runs on the printer. A word is considered long if it has seven or more letters. A long-word run consists of one or more consecutive long words. Only long-word runs containing three or more words are saved in the results. Here too, the program prints out a page number and line number so that you can quickly locate the long-word runs.

Proceed as follows to print out a list of all long-word runs:

- Check that the printer is ON-LINE (ready for printing).
- Press **F2**.

When printing is finished, you can leave this submenu:

- Press **Esc**.

8 Tips

You can call up a number of useful tips for each of the result displays that you look at. Sometimes these tips consist of ideal values that you can compare with your own writing. Sometimes you obtain tips on how to improve your writing. If you wish to look at the tips:

- Press **F8**.

When you have finished reading the tips:

- Press **Esc**.

9 Ideal

An ideal display is available for each result display that you look at. To compare your result display with the ideal display, proceed as follows:

- Press **F9**.

When you have finished looking at the ideal display:

- Press **Esc**.

10 Help

Your Readability program has a built-in help function (**F10**) which provides you with brief, helpful information as your work proceeds.

- Press **F10**.

When you have finished with the help information:

- Press **Esc**.

Selecting a result display

To select a result display, you must respond to the following prompt:

```
Desired display:_
```

If you know which display you wish to look at and you know its number:

- Type the display's number.
- Press the ↵ key.

If you do not which display you wish to look at or if you are uncertain about its number:

- Press **F4**.

You can now look through a list of the displays that are available. When you have decided which one you wish to look at:

- Type the display's number.
- Press the ↵ key.

Browsing among the displays

You can also browse among the different displays by pressing **PgDn** and **PgUp**.

PgDn moves you forward to the next display.

PgUp moves you back to the previous display.

Explanation of the different result displays

The different result displays are explained below. Remember that you can always call up useful tips via the submenu or call up the ideal displays. More information about how to interpret the results is presented in the chapter entitled *How to improve readability*.

In this tutorial, we will use part of the first chapter from Tom Sawyer by Mark Twain as an example that provides good analysis results. Naturally, your writing doesn't always have to resemble Tom Sawyer, but even if you are writing for adults and dealing with more complicated subjects than rafting down the Mississippi, it might be a good idea to use a similar writing style. If you wish to look at the result displays while you are reading this chapter, proceed as follows:

- Start Readability.
- Press **F3** to look at the results of a previous analysis.
- Highlight SAWYER.
- Press the ↵ key.

The STYLE diagram for the requested text will now appear.

Display 11 – Style diagram

Display 11 consists of the style diagram for the text in question. On this diagram, each sentence in the text is represented by a dot. The computer positions these dots on the basis the number of words in the sentence and also on how many long words each sentence contains. A word is considered long if it has more than six letters.

The ideal curve shows the ideal relationship between sentence length and number of long words per sentence. The ideal curve is shown on the style diagram by means of very small points (considerably smaller than the dots used to represent analyzed sentences).

An asterisk (*) indicates the focal point of the text on the diagram.

Preferably, the sentences (dots) should be spread evenly to the left and to the right of the ideal curve so that the focal point falls on or close to the ideal curve. Most of the sentences should lie within pattern 1 (normal diagram).

An easy-to-read text has numerous sentences near the bottom of the diagram. This means that many sentences contain only short words. Note that the sentences in the Sawyer diagram are arranged in such a pattern.

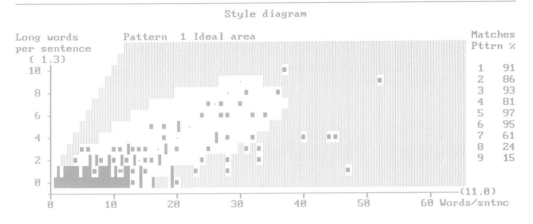

```
C:SAWYER    Tom Sawyer by Mark Twain                    Display: 111
                          Style diagram
Long words        Pattern  1 Ideal area                    Matches
per sentence                                               Pttrn %
 ( 1.3)
   10                                                        1    91
                                                             2    86
    8                                                        3    93
                                                             4    81
    6                                                        5    97
                                                             6    95
    4                                                        7    61
                                                             8    24
    2                                                        9    15
    0
                                                        (11.0)
     0      10      20      30      40      50      60 Words/sntnc
```

As you can see from this illustration, the Sawyer sentences are located on both sides of the ideal curve. The focal point is located at 11.0/1.3 which is slightly to the right of the ideal curve. Good. There are only three sentences in the upper left-hand area (where complicated sentences are plotted). Very good. Several sentences have been plotted out to the right in the area used for wordy and pompous sentences. If you press **F6**, move the cursor to the right-most sentence and press the ↵ key, you will see that the 105th sentence in the text is located there.

To obtain some idea of what this type of writing resembles most, proceed as follows:

- Study the percentages in the column to the right of the style diagram and see which pattern had the highest percentage of matches for this text.

- Press **F8** to see what the different patterns are called: Select the desired pattern with the arrow keys or by typing in the pattern number to see how well the text in question matches the selected pattern.

Displays 111–119 (Style diagrams)

Displays 111–119 (like display 11) are STYLE diagrams for the text. Display 11 is for the pattern that you selected when you conducted the analysis. Displays 111–119 permit you to look at the same information plotted onto the different patterns.

Display 12 – Sentence characteristics

Each sentence in the text is classified as one of the following types, which are defined om page 6–7.

- Simple
- Normal
- Narrative
- Foggy
- Wordy
- Elegant
- Difficult
- Pompous
- Complicated

Normal, foggy and difficult sentences lie between the ideal curve and the warning curve. This latter is explained in the chapter entitled *How Readability was created*. Simple, narrative and elegant sentences are located to the right of the ideal curve.

Display 12 shows the percentages of each type of sentence in the text in question. The spread around the focal point is a measure of the extent to which the sentences are spread in the style diagram.

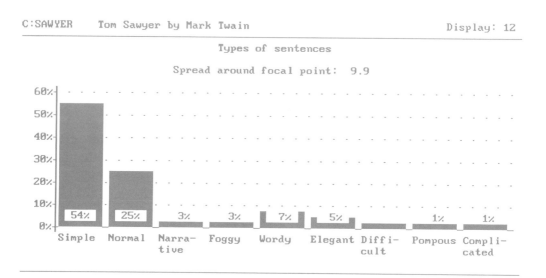

The Sawyer text contains mostly simple and normal sentences. It is easy to read. The spread around the focal point is greater than 8, which is good. The bars on the diagram get shorter as one moves to the right, and this complies with the pattern found in the ideal display (press **F9**). The text contains only 1 % complicated sentences. However there are 7 % wordy sentences.

Display 13 – Long words per sentence

Display 13 presents the number of long words per sentence. If you use too many long words, your writing is difficult to read, especially if you do not use many small words to "dilute" the text. If possible, avoid using more than nine long words in a single sentence.

You can find out how many sentences have a specified number of long words or more. If, for example, you wish to find out how many sentences have five or more long words:

• Type:

  5 –

• Press the ↵ key.

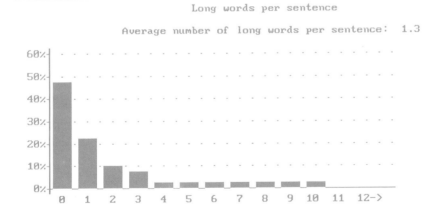

The display showing the number of long words per sentence for the Sawyer text sets a good example for easy-to-read writing. Most of the sentences contain 0, 1 and 2 long words. The smooth profile of the bars on the diagram indicates that the language used was written by a single person. In situations where a number of people have written or edited a text, the pattern is usually more irregular.

Display 14 – Sentence lengths

Fig. 14 presents the number of words per sentence. People often believe mistakenly that easy-to-read writing consists of short sentences. However, the results provided by your Readability program show that just the opposite is often true. Easy-to-read writing can contain long sentences if the number of long words per sentence is kept low. The upper limit for sentence length is about 35 words.

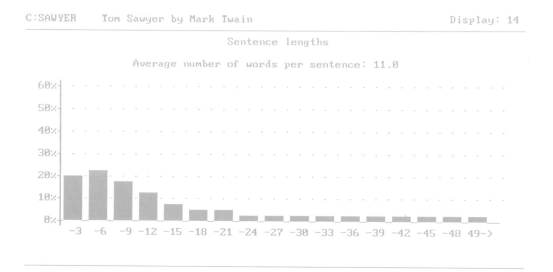

```
C:SAWYER    Tom Sawyer by Mark Twain                           Display: 14

                        Sentence lengths

          Average number of words per sentence: 11.0
   60%
   50%
   40%
   30%
   20%
   10%
    0%
        -3  -6  -9 -12 -15 -18 -21 -24 -27 -30 -33 -36 -39 -42 -45 -48 49->
```

Display 14 shows that Mark Twain did not hesitate to write long sentences.

You can find out how many sentences have more than a specified number of words. If, for example, you wish to know what sentences contain 35 or more words, proceed as follows:

- Type:

    35-

- Press the ↵ key.

Display 15 – Consecutive short words

The more short words you write in succession, the easier it will be for your reader to grasp your meaning. Display 15 presents the number of consecutive short words.

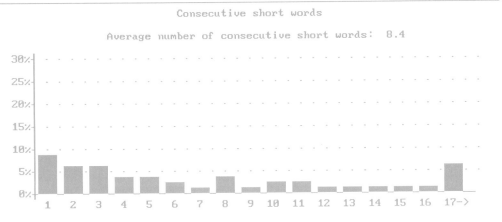

C:SAWYER   Tom Sawyer by Mark Twain   Display: 15

Consecutive short words

Average number of consecutive short words: 8.4

As you can see, the Sawyer text has many short words in succession. This improves readability. Only about 8 % of the short-word runs contain only a single word.

Display 16 – Consecutive long words

When you write texts containing numerous facts that force you to use long words, it is important that you avoid the use of long long-word runs.

Display 16 shows the number of consecutive long words. You can find out how many runs having a specified number of long words were used in the text by specifying the desired run length followed by a hyphen.

If, for example, you wish to look at long-word runs which contain three or more long words in succession, proceed as follows:

- Type:

  3 -

- Press the ↵ key.

The first 3-long-word run in the text will now appear.

- If you press the ↵ key repeatedly, you can look at subsequent runs.

5 - 13

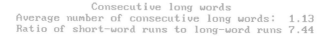

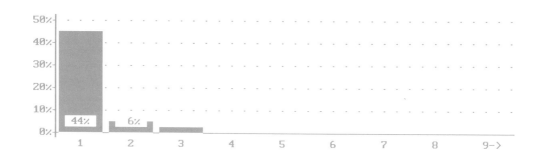

The display shows that 44 % of the runs contain a single long word. This indicates that many long words are surrounded by short words. Such a configuration is extremely easy to read! The fact that the ratio of short-word runs to long-word runs is 7.44 indicates that the text contains many short-word runs. Even 3.5 would have been a good value.

Display 21 – Word lengths

The words in the text being examined are divided into groups based on length. This display shows the percentages of words containing 1–2 letters, 3–4 letters, . . . , 17 or more letters.

You can find out how many words of a specified length were used. If, for example, you wish to find out how many bricks had 14 or more letters:

● Type:

   14-

● Press the ◄┘ key.

If you want to find out how many words had precisely four letters:

● Type:

   -4-

● Press the ◄┘ key.

If you want to find out how many words had 3–4 letters inclusive:

- Type:

  `3-4`

- Press the ⏎ key.

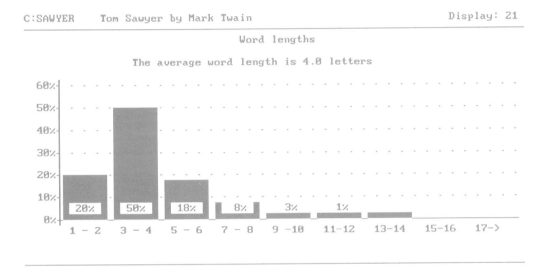

C:SAWYER   Tom Sawyer by Mark Twain   Display: 21

Word lengths

The average word length is 4.0 letters

The word lengths in the Sawyer texts averaged 4.0 letters (a low and thus good value). The text did not contain a single word longer than 14 letters. That's one of the reasons why it's so easy to read.

Display 22 – Bricks

When your Readability program analyzes a text, it keeps a record of all the different words and how often they have been used.

In display 22, the program has segregated the 400 most frequently used words in the English language. The remaining words (called bricks) are presented in a list which also tells you how many times each of these words was used.

```
C:SAWYER     Tom Sawyer by Mark Twain                        Display: 22

                            564     bricks
     30   TOM                              4   WHAT'S
     10   I'LL                             4   YES
      9   CAN'T                            3   ANYBODY
      8   YOU'RE                           3   BIT
      7   AUNT                             3   BLACK
      6   AIN'T                            3   CHILD
      5   KNOW                             3   CLOTHES
      5   LICK                             3   COLLAR
      4   BROTHER                          3   DUST
      4   DARE                             3   HIT
      4   I'VE                             3   HEART
      4   OH                               3   HOOKEY
      4   SHIRT                            3   JIM
      4   SAYING                           3   JACKET
      4   THAT'S                           3   LADY
      4   TOM'S                            3   LEARN

                                                   Press ⏎
```

As you can see, the most frequently used bricks in the Sawyer texts were Tom (30 times) and aunt (7) times.

To browse forward in this list:

- Press the ⏎ key.

Here, you can find all of the bricks that begin in a certain way. If you wish to look at all bricks in the Sawyer text that begin with "res":

- Type:

  res

- Press the ⏎ key.

Moreover, you can find all the bricks that end in a specified series of letters. If, for example, you wish to look at all the bricks that end in "ing":

- Type:

  ing

- Press the ⏎ key.

You can also find all of the bricks having a specified minimum number of letters. If, for example, you wish to look at all of the bricks that have at least 13 letters:

- Type:

  13-

- Press the ↵ key.

Moreover, you can find all of the words which (for example) have a maximum of 5 letters:

- Type:

  -5

- Press the ↵ key.

And finally, you can combine all four of the above. If, for example, you wish to find all of the words that begin with "s" and have between 4 and 7 letters inclusive:

- Type:

  4-7 s

- Press the ↵ key.

If you, for example, want to find all of the words that end in "ing" and have at least 11 letters:

- Type:

  11-   -ing

- Press the ↵ key.

Remember, however, that the 400 most frequently used words in the English language were eliminated before making the above analyses.

Display 23 – Mortar and bricks

The 400 most frequently used words are called mortar. All other words are called bricks. Usually, a text contains around 40 % bricks. If this percentage is higher, it indicates that more difficult words have been selected in your text than in a normal text.

Display 23 shows the percentages of bricks and mortar.

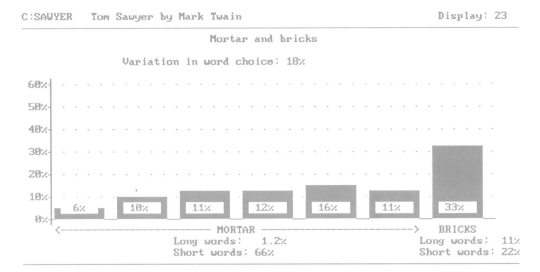

C:SAWYER   Tom Sawyer by Mark Twain   Display: 23

Mortar and bricks

Variation in word choice: 18%

For the Sawyer text, display 23 shows that there is a favorable ratio between mortar and bricks. This text has only 31 % bricks which is somewhat high for a book intended for young people. This 31 % was divided up as follows: 10 % short bricks, 20 % long bricks (long = more than six letters), and 1 % reading error.

Display 24 – Comments on choice of words

If your Readability program has any comments to make on the words you've used in the text, they are presented in display 24.

The comments in display 24 are based on the list of synonyms that is included with your Readability program. This list is in a file named SYNLIST.RDB (located on your program diskette). More information about this file is presented in the section headed *List of synonyms*.

The Readability program did not find any reason to make comments on the Sawyer text. As a result, display 24 appears as follows:

C:SAWYER   Tom Sawyer by Mark Twain   Display: 24

Comments on word selection

Words	Comments
CALCULATED	likely?
PRODUCED	make
PECULIAR	odd
RUINATION	ruin

Display 31 – Sentence characteristics

Display 31 shows how each sentence has been evaluated, starting from the beginning of the text and proceeding sentence by sentence. Here, you can easily see which sentences are "narrative" and which are "difficult". You should compare this with the characteristic breakdowns presented in displays 11 and 12. If, in spite of their disadvantages, you must include complicated sentences in your writing, you should make every effort to prevent them from being bunched together. This also applies to pompous and wordy sentences.

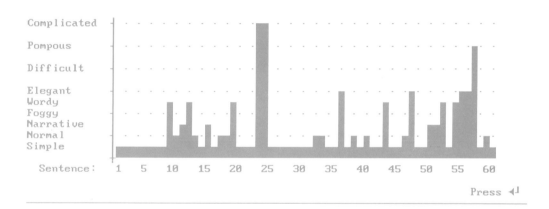

If a text consists of more than 60 sentences, you can browse forward as follows:

- Press the ↵ key.

You can find all of the deviant sentences (those which lie outside the area covered by the teardrop outline). If, for example, you wish to look at all deviant sentences starting with sentence No. 10:

- Type:

  10-

- Press the ↵ key.

You are now provided with information about the first deviant sentence. To look at the next (and then the next, etc.), proceed as follows:

- Press the ↵ key repeatedly.

Display 32 – Long words per sentence

Display 32 presents the number of long words per sentence. Here too, you can find the deviant sentences.

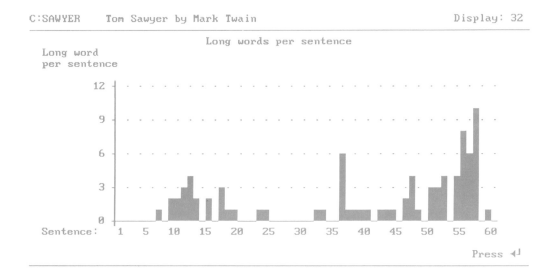

```
C:SAWYER     Tom Sawyer by Mark Twain                        Display: 32
```
Long words per sentence

```
Long word
per sentence
        12
         9
         6
         3
         0
Sentence:   1   5  10  15  20  25  30  35  40  45  50  55  60
```
Press ↵

The number of long words per sentence varies considerably in the Sawyer text. There is only one sentence containing more than nine long words. Groups of sentences containing long words are mostly scattered widely.

If a text contains more than 60 sentences, you can browse forward:

- Press the ↵ key.

You can find all deviant sentences. If you wish to look at all deviant sentences starting with sentence No. 10:

- Type:

  10-

- Press the ↵ key.

You are now provided with information about the first deviant sentence. To look at the next (and then the next, etc.), proceed as follows:

- Press the ↵ key repeatedly.

Display 33 – Sentence lengths

Display 33 shows how long each sentence is, starting at the beginning of the text and proceeding forward sentence by sentence. As a result, you can easily see how successful you have been in varying sentence length throughout the text.

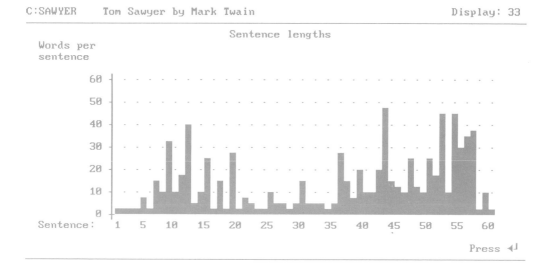

In the Sawyer text, sentence length varies considerably, although you can find examples of long sentences that are bunched together. Text in which sentences of varying lengths are well scattered captures and retains a reader's interest.

If a text contains more than 60 sentences, you can browse forward:

- Press the ↵ key.

Display 41 – General evaluation

Display 41 presents a general evaluation of the text. This evaluation is based on six factors:

- **Focal point distance** – the distance from the average point in the sentence distribution to the ideal curve
- **Spread relative to focal point** – the degree to which the sentences are distributed around the focal point
- **Compliance with the ideal curve** – the degree to which the sentences are located near the ideal curve
- **Readability Index** – the level of difficulty based upon the average number of words in each sentence and the average number of long words per sentence
- **Percentage of mortar** – the percent of words found on the list of the 400 most common English words
- **Short word sentences** – the percentage of sentences containing only short words (under 7 letters)

Each factor can be compared with the ideal factors. To compare the different factors, you must invoke Tips and Ideal on the submenu.

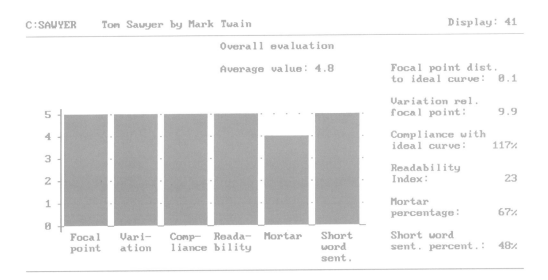

Any writer could be proud of a general evaluation as good as that earned by the Sawyer text. The figure 117 % for compliance with the ideal curve indicates that, viewed as a whole, the sentences are somewhat to the right of the ideal curve.

Display 42 – General comments

This display presents you with advice on how to improve your writing with regard to the percentage of long words per sentence, the number of words per sentence and the spread of the sentences on the style diagram. The following comments are provided for the Sawyer text:

```
C:SAWYER    Tom Sawyer by Mark Twain                     Display: 42
                          General comments
  * Text's focal point is very favorably located.

  * Text has a broad spread on the Style diagram. Very Good!

  * Text contains a high percentage of sentences containing only
    short words. Easy to read!
  * Text contains many simple words. Easy to understand.


  You can improve text's readability by:

  - eliminate all "complicated" sentences
```

Display 43 – Number of sentences and words

Display 43 presents the following numeric data:

- Number of characters in text.

- Number of words in text and how many are short and long.

- Number of sentences in text.

- Average number of words per sentence and how many of them are (on the average) short and long.

Display 43 appears as follows for the Sawyer text:

```
C:SAWYER    Tom Sawyer by Mark Twain                          Display: 43
                        Number of  sentences  and  words

   Numbers of characters in text: 9617

   Number of words: 2413 of which 2127 are short and 286 are long.

   Number of sentences: 220

   On the average each sentences contain: 11.0 words of which
                                           9.7 are short and 1.3 are long.
```

List of synonyms

Display 24, which presents comments on the words that have been selected, is based on a list of synonyms included as part of the Readability program. This list of synonyms is in a file named SYN-LIST.RDB, and it is on your program diskette.

Installing a list of synonyms

If you have DOS version 3.0 or later, it is advisable to put the list of synonyms in the same subdirectory and disk drive as the Readability program. However, you can also put the list of synonyms in the subdirectory that is active when you start the program. You will find the DOS version number on the DOS diskette that came with your computer.

If your version of DOS is earlier (lower) than 3.0, you can put the list of synonyms in the directory that is active when you start the program.

Note that this also applies to lists of synonyms that you yourself create.

Changing SYNLIST.RDB

You can use any word processing program which writes or converts to ASCII to add words to or remove words from the list of synonyms.

You may wish to add words in order to:

- Avoid using them.
- Remember explanations.

When you use a word that is in the list of synonyms, you obtain comments on it in display 24.

The list of synonyms does not have any effect on your text. This means that any words that you wish to avoid are not eliminated automatically. However, you are reminded of whether or not you should use a particular word. To make a change in a list of synonyms, proceed as follows (for example):

- Start the word processing program.
- Load the program called:

```
synlist.rdb
```

After you have started the word processing program and loaded (retrieved) SYNLIST.RDB, you can add or delete synonyms to or from the list using the ordinary word processing procedures.

To make a change, proceed as follows:

- Use upper case letters for the keywords.
- Enter the # character (if you do not have it on your regular keyboard hold Alt down and type 35 using the keys on the numeric keypad) immediately after the word in order to search for a synonym.
- Type a space immediately after the word in order to search for a word whose first letters are the same.

For each keyword you can type a comment containing a maximum of 40 characters. You can write these using lower case letters.

Example:

REGISTER#   Searches for the word "register" in your text.

STATION   Searches for all words that start with station.

A part of SYNLIST might appear as follows:

PURCHASE buy, shop
RECORD# enter (into)
DEPOSIT save
ACQUIRE get
PROCURE buy

Note!
You must save SYNLIST.RDB as a non-document.

Creating your own lists of synonyms

You can have different lists of synonyms for different types of text.

You create these lists as ordinary word processing program documents, as set forth above. However, you must save each list as a ASCII file. Remember to select names for your synonym lists that are meaningful so that you can retrieve them easily.

Activating one of your own lists of synonyms

You can activate one of your own lists of synonyms by typing its name when you start Readability. If the desired list of synonyms was named MYLIST.RDB, proceed as follows to change to it:

- Type:

```
rdb s=c:mylist.rdb
```

- Press the ↵ key.

Basic Readability concepts

In this chapter, we will review the basic concepts of the Readability method and the factors you will encounter in your Readability program.

What and how does Readability measure?

When we speak, we are able to watch our listener and observe his reactions. This is not true when we write. Your Readability program gives you some idea of how readable a reader will find your writing.

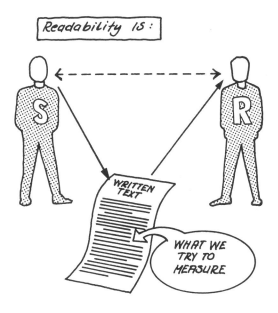

The Readability method is based on statistical procedures that measure word length, sentence length, percentage of commonly encountered words.

Naturally, there are many other factors that affect the ease with which a reader can understand whatever message we are trying to get across. For example, your Readability program has no way of knowing how familiar the reader is with the subject at hand, how interested he is in it or his general level of education. Syntax errors that flaw the structure of a sentence and unclear references within sentences are also examples of factors that your Readability program cannot measure. However, it nonetheless provides you with a useful and objective measure of the quality of your writing.

One can say that a good Readability rating is a necessary but not all-embracing evaluation of a piece of writing.

While creating Readability, Roland Larson analyzed approximately 600,000 words in texts taken from many different fields. These analyses showed that texts which we consider easy to read earn good Readability ratings, while texts that people consider difficult to read and difficult to understand fail to earn good ratings. One example of good writing is the excerpt from Tom Sawyer by Mark Twain used as an example in this manual.

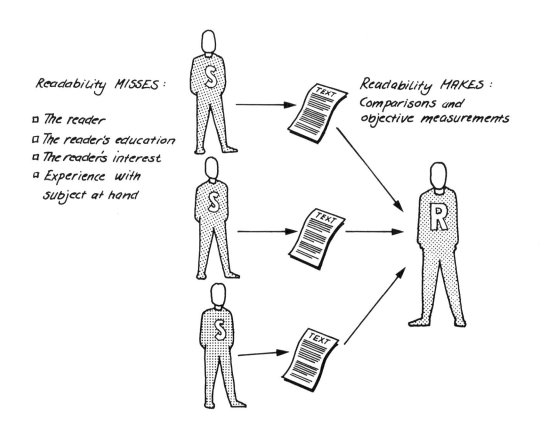

Readability MISSES:

☐ *The reader*
☐ *The reader's education*
☐ *The reader's interest*
☐ *Experience with subject at hand*

Readability MAKES:
Comparisons and objective measurements

Language building blocks

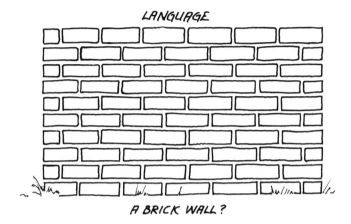

A BRICK WALL?

Writing can be compared with building a brick wall. Here, the bricks form the wall itself, but in order to join them together, you must use plenty of mortar. The ratio of bricks to mortar must be properly balanced in a stable, well-built wall.

In language, we use many small words and bridging words that serve as mortar. All other words are considered bricks.

Your Readability program contains the 400 most frequently used words in the English language. They are considered mortar, and all other words are considered bricks.

Bricks

Bricks are the words that carry the information we wish to convey. The following are examples of bricks:

snowstorm, twilight, television, chimney, computer

Any sentence that contains more than nine bricks will very probably be difficult to understand.

Mortar

Mortar comprises the small words which, in and of themselves, do not carry very much information, but nonetheless lend life to language and make it easy to understand. The following are examples of mortar:

come, that, one, as, and, if, had, an, in

Both short and long words serve as mortar, but most mortar words are shorter than bricks.

If you want your writing to be pleasant and easy to read, you must use plenty of mortar. In good writing, bricks and mortar are properly balanced. A sentence that contains too many bricks will be somewhat foggy and perhaps complicated. A sentence having too much mortar will be wordy. However, situations arise in which a sentence containing only short words is needed to provide a "break" in the text so that the reader will be able to recover his capacity to digest highly informative sentences.

Readability measures the ratio of bricks to mortar and, if they're properly balanced, issues a good rating.

Commonly used words

The 400 most commonly used words in the English language are its mortar. What are these words? Let's take a look at the most frequently used:

FREQUENCY WORD LIST

WORD LENGTH	RANK	WORD
1	5	A
2	2	OF
3	1	THE
4	7	THAT
5	31	WHICH
6	90	BEFORE
7	92	THROUGH

The most frequently used words are short. Among the 100 most frequently used words, there is only one that is longer than six letters. This is the word "through" which is in 92nd place.

What percentage of a text is normally made up of commonly used words? The following throw some light on this question.

- The two most frequently used words (the, of) make up about 10 % of a text.

- The six most frequently used words make up about 20 % of a text.

- The 400 most frequently used words make up about 60 % of a text.

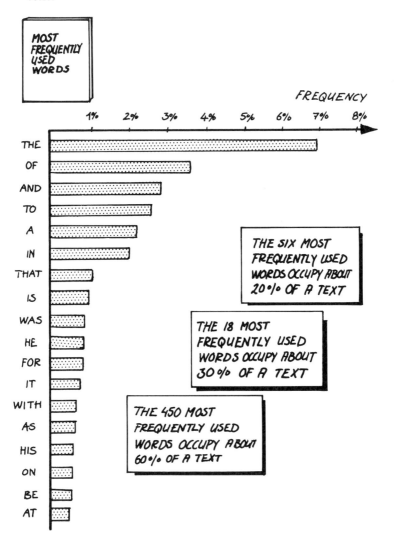

Misconception about sentence length

People often conclude mistakenly that short sentences are needed for good readability. However, short sentences must not become an objective in and of themselves. There is no reason not to write long sentences (although not too long). Mixing short and long sentences together is good practice. However, it is important to note that sentences should not contain too many long words.

Style diagram

In the Readability method, there is no risk that different poor ratings will cancel out each other. Your Readability program assigns each sentence a dot on the style diagram. The locations of the dots on the diagram provide a graphic indication of the characteristics of a text.

This serves as the basis of the style diagram.

Your Readability program measures the number of words and the number of long words in each sentence. (A long word is a word having seven or more letters.)

Each sentence is assigned a characteristic (name) depending on where it is located in the style diagram.

- **Simple** – a short sentence made up almost entirely of short words
- **Normal** – a short sentence containing a few long words
- **Narrative** – a medium length sentence containing a few long words
- **Foggy** – a medium length sentence with several long words
- **Elegant** – a fairly long sentence with several long words
- **Difficult** – a fairly long sentence with a lot of long words
- **Complicated** – a fairly long sentence with too many long words to be easily understood
- **Pompous** – a sentence with too many words to be easily understood, and which usually has too many long words as well
- **Wordy** – a sentence with too many words to be easily understood, but which has relatively few long words.

Ideal area on the style diagram

When you analyze a text, you select the pattern against which you want your sentences to be evaluated. Your Readability program has nine patterns for different types of texts (newspaper article and technical manuals to cite two examples).

Each sentence that falls outside the teardrop outline in the selected pattern is classified by the program as deviant. These deviant sentences are of particular interest to you, since they do not comply with the intended type of writing.

Your Readability program permits you to look at all deviant sentences very conveniently. You'll see on the screen the beginnings of the sentences and their locations in the text. If you have a printer connected to your computer, you can also print out a list of all deviant sentences. Here too, you will be provided with information that enables you to find them quickly in the text.

Good writing requires sentence variation. Long and short sentences should be interspersed and they should contain different numbers of long words. The ideal area on the style diagram contains the following types of sentences: normal, simple, foggy, narrative, difficult and elegant. Sentences that are wordy, complicated and pompous fall outside the ideal area.

The style diagram's ideal area appears as follows:

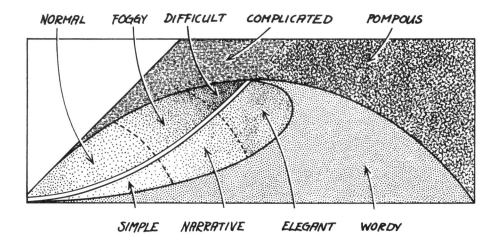

How to improve readability

In this chapter, we shall discuss the things that can lower your Readability Index and thus improve your writing.

We shall take a look at the types of mistakes that can disturb the flow of language and the effects that they have on sentence characteristics.

Readability detects and measures symptoms

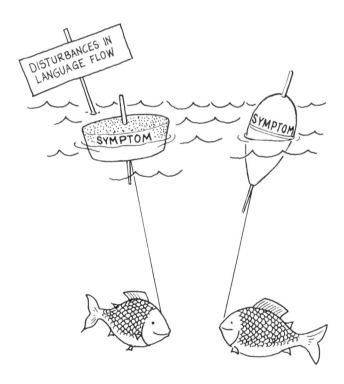

Readability finds and measures shoals in the sea of language. Excessively long sentences indicate that something is wrong. Complicated, difficult, pompous or wordy sentences indicate that something else is wrong. But what? This chapter presents examples of the things that can lead to undesired results.

Language flow contaminants

There are many things that can disturb language flow, and either alone or in combination they skew our sentences into the upper left-hand part of the style diagram.

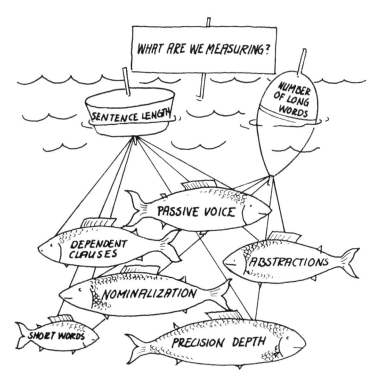

Nominalization

Here, the writer shows an unfortunate tendency to turn verbs into nouns. Sentences constructed in this way tend to obscure the writer's message somewhat and should be avoided. For example, we might write:

Sam formulated a number of word abbreviations.

It would have been better if we had written:

Sam abbreviated a number of words.

By switching the meaning of the word "abbreviation" from a noun to a verb we made the sentence easier to read. Needless nominalization (using nouns in situations where verbs are more concise) detracts from clarity.

Passive voice

We can express things in either passive or active voice. For example, we can say, "Tom Sawyer was written by Mark Twain", or "Mark Twain wrote Tom Sawyer". Bureaucratic gobbledygook is full of sentences constructed using the passive voice. For example:

Pressure gauges are utilized to measure tire pressure.

It would be better to write:

Pressure gauges measure tire pressure.

By avoiding a passive structure, we made the sentence easier to understand. In a passive construction, the object becomes the center of interest instead of whatever it is that acts on it.

Excessive details

We can complicate our sentences needlessly by using too much detail. If someone asks you whether he should take an umbrella along when he goes out to lunch, there is no reason to give him a full weather report.

Abstractions

Abstractions are another form of disturbance that complicate sentences needlessly. Let's take a really bad example:

Unstructured document archives generate serious accessibility problems.

This means:

I can't find my papers when my desk is in a mess.

Another example:

There is every reason to strive for uncomplicated sentence structures in order to enhance the readability.

This means:

Use a simple style if you want people to get your message.

Is there ever any good reason to write something that is abstract? Only if you wish to impress someone. But even here, there's considerable doubt about the matter. What impresses people most is clear, concise writing. A readable text impresses everyone in the right way.

If your writing is abstract, it will contain too many complicated sentences, and perhaps even a few that are pompous.

Status enhancement

Sometimes, we feel that it is necessary to seek "status" in our text. We believe that if we use simple, everyday words we won't be making the right impression. We write entrance or doorway instead of door.

For example:

He is given to prevarication.

Instead of:

He is a clever liar.

Other examples:

The public – Media consumers

Drunks – Alcohol intensive individuals

Laundry – Cleanup facility

Prolonging words

Sometimes, we are tempted to prolong words in order to make them sound more impressive. For example:

Typical – Prototypical

Oriented – Orientated

Communicate – Intercommunicate

Status-enhancing jargon

Here, our decisions must be based partly on our target group and even on the extent to which jargon has found its way into everyday usage. The word "database" for example would not have had much meaning five years ago. Today, however, many target groups are thoroughly familiar with it.

You should thus write:

To stay healthy, we need simple food and plenty of exercise.

Instead of:

Preserving bodily well-being requires an uncomplicated diet combined with adequate physical exertion.

You should write:

It is nice to live in a house with a good view.

Instead of:

Dwellings that overlook attractive scenic panoramas provide aesthetic gratification.

Dependent clause

A dependent clause rides piggyback on the main sentence. In the following example no dependent clause is used:

My car sometimes refuses to start in the mornings. It is old and worn out.

If we were to use a dependent clause, this would read:

My car, which is old and worn out, sometimes refuses to start in the mornings.

Dependent clauses increase sentence length and often lead to the use of too many long words per sentence. Readers thus get confused.

Judicious use of dependent clauses

It's not always wrong to use a dependent clause. Sometimes you can use them to spruce up your text. Authors of novels often use dependent clauses.

Long sentences do not detract from readability in and of themselves, but they should not contain too many long words. Good writing contains both long and short sentences.

How disturbances show up on the STYLE diagram and displays

This section will explain how language-flow contaminants affect the STYLE diagram and displays.

STYLE diagram

A text's style diagram provides you with a clear picture of how your sentences are spread around the focal point. It also shows how many sentences fall inside and outside the ideal area. If many sentences are outside the ideal area, your style diagram is giving you a warning.

Writing that is skewed upward and to the left on the style diagram is foggy and perhaps even complicated. Sentences located in the upper right-hand part of the diagram are pompous. Such sentences should always be avoided. Sentences in the lower right-hand part of the diagram are wordy. Perhaps you didn't really know what you wanted to say in these sentences.

Remember that the style diagram indicates the specific sentences that were deviant (outside the ideal area). By pressing **F6**, you can take a look at any desired deviant sentence.

You can also print out a list of all deviant sentences on your printer by first pressing **F7** and then **F1**.

Analysis pattern 1

Theoretically, analysis pattern 1 is the normal diagram. The other analysis patterns are more specific. They are based on the results of numerous analyses that have been conducted.

Sentence characteristics

Display 12 (sentence characteristics) shows the percentages of the different types of sentences of each type you have written. The Readability program recognizes nine types. They are listed on page 6–7.

- A simple sentence is quite short and contains short words.

- A complicated sentence is quite short and contains many long words.

- A wordy sentence is long and contains only a few long words.

- A pompous sentence is long and contains many long words.

The bar representing normal sentences should be the highest. You should also have many simple and narrative sentences. Try to avoid too many wordy, elegant or difficult sentences. Preferably, there should not be any pompous or complicated sentences.

Sentences that are normal, simple, foggy, narrative, difficult and elegant fall within the ideal area on the style diagram. Sentences that are wordy, complicated or pompous fall outside this ideal area.

Display 31 presents a graphic picture on which you can see each sentence of each type. This display also shows the extent to which you varied sentence structure in your text.

Troubleshooting

If you have too many foggy or complicated sentences, it may mean that you are using:

- Nominalization

- Abstractions

- Status enhancement

You will find examples of the above at the beginning of this chapter.

If your text includes pompous sentences, it may mean that you are using:

Abstractions

Excessive detail

You will find examples of the above at the beginning of this chapter.

Have headings etc. been eliminated?

Headings and the like can distort your results and they should thus be eliminated. Headings that have not been eliminated are chained to the sentences that follow them, and as a result you may have too many long sentences and too many long words per sentence. Tables included in your text can also distort the results.

This is because your Readability program defines the end of sentences as follows:

- Periods followed by upper case letters.
- Question marks followed by upper case letters.
- Explanation points followed by upper case letters.
- Colons followed by upper case letters.
- Semicolons.

The chapter entitled *How to analyze a text* explains how to eliminate the appropriate parts of your text from the analysis.

Spread around the focal point

Display 12 presents a value that indicates the extent to which your sentences are spread around the focal point. This shows how varied your sentences are. If this value is as low as 4, your sentence structures are probably too monotonous.

If you vary the structures of your sentences, your language will be livelier, and this will tend to capture and hold the reader's interest.

Long words per sentence

Display 13 presents a diagram of the number of long words per sentence in your text.

Words having more than six letters are considered long. Most of your sentences should not contain more than three long words. Sentences containing only short words (0 long words) help your readers digest highly informative parts of your text.

It is important that you maintain a proper relationship between sentence length and number of long words per sentence. If you find yourself in a situation where you are forced to use many long words in a single sentence, try to "pad" them with short words so that they will be easier to comprehend.

```
    —•RECIPE•—
LONG
WORDS      SENTENCE LENGTH
PER
SENTENCE SHORTEST IDEAL LONGEST

  1:        2 __ 10 ___ 18
  2:        4 ___ 14 ___ 24
  3:        6 ___ 17 ___ 28
  4:        8 __ 20 ___ 32
  5:       10 __ 22 ___ 34
  6:       13 __ 24 ___ 35
  7:       16 __ 26 ___ 36
  8:     20 __ 28 ___ 36
  9:     27 __ 30 ___ 33
 10:     SHOULD BE
         AVOIDED !
```

Display 32 shows, sentence by sentence, how the numbers of long words per sentence vary throughout your text. It also shows the extent to which you were able to vary your sentence structures.

Troubleshooting

If you have many long words per sentence, it may be because you are using:

- Abstractions

- Status enhancement

- Excessive detail

You will find examples of the above at the beginning of this chapter.

Sentence lengths

Display 14 shows the lengths of the sentences used in your text graphically.

There is no reason not to write long sentences, but you shouldn't put too many long words in them. Vary the lengths of your sentences, but avoid those that are longer than 35 words. Varying sentence lengths is important since it will impart life to your writing and capture the reader's interest.

Display 33 shows how long your sentences are, on a sentence-by-sentence basis. Here, you can see how well you succeeded in varying sentence length. See to it that long sentences are not too close to each other.

Troubleshooting

If you have too many long sentences, it may be because you have used:

- Excessive detail

- Dependent clauses

You will find examples of the above at the beginning of this chapter.

Consecutive short words

Display 15 shows the short-word runs in your text graphically.

Many consecutive short words enhance readability!

If the leftmost bar in display 15 is higher than 15 %, it indicates that you are using a single short word between long words too frequently. Use more short, commonly used words.

Consecutive long words

Display 16 presents the long-word runs in your text graphically.

Many consecutive long words (a run) make your writing heavy and difficult to read. About 40 % of the long words you use should be interspersed with short words and you should always try to avoid putting more than two long words next to each other.

Troubleshooting

If your writing has too many consecutive long words, it may be because you are using too few short, frequently used words.

You may also have used:

- Abstractions

- Status enhancement

- Excessive detail

You will find examples of the above at the beginning of this chapter.

Display 16 also presents the ratio of short-word runs to long-word runs. This ratio should be as high as possible, preferably more than 3.5. The program calculates this ratio by dividing the average number of words in a short-word run by the average number of words in a long-word run.

Printing out a list of long-word runs

You can print out a list of all of the long-word runs in your text on your printer. First press **F7** and then **F2**.

Word lengths

Display 21 presents the word lengths used in your text graphically.

Do not use long words unless necessary. They are hard to read. You should not use words longer than 12 letters, and only a few percent should be longer than 8 letters.

Troubleshooting

If your text contains too many long words, you may have used:

- Abstractions

- Status enhancement

- Excessive detail

- Passive voice

You will find examples of the above at the beginning of this chapter.

Bricks

The 400 most frequently words in the English language are called mortar. All other words are bricks. Bricks are the words used to carry essential information.

Display 22 presents the bricks that you have used and tells you how many times you have used them.

Mortar and bricks

Display 23 presents a graphic picture of the relationship between mortar and bricks in your text.

The 400 most frequently used words comprise 60 % of normal text. If the rightmost bar (bricks) is higher than 40 %, the words you have selected for your text are more difficult than normal.

You must use a great deal of mortar – short, frequently used words – to make your text more readable.

Word variation

You should vary the words in your text so that you will capture and then retain your reader's interest. If the words you select are not sufficiently varied, your text will be dull and monotonous. Your word choice should vary by 18 %-20 %. Word variation is calculated as the ratio of the number of bricks that appear only once in your text to the total number of words in the text.

Comments on word choice

The program runs through all of the bricks in your text to see whether you have used any words that are not suitable. These may be words that involve status enhancement. The program can also pick out other words of doubtful content and words that require comments.

The comments in display 24 are based on the list of synonyms called SYNLIST.RDB which is included with your Readability program. You can add words to this list. You can have different lists of synonyms for different types of text. You specify the one you want to use when you start your Readability program.

You can read more about SYNLIST.RDB and about creating your own lists of synonyms in the section headed *List of synonyms*.

General evaluation

Display 41 presents a general evaluation of your text.

This display shows an average rating that can range from 0 to 5. If your rating is between 4 and 5, you should be very proud of your work since a rating of 2 or 3 is considered good. On the other hand, if your rating is lower than 2, you should take a close look at the six bars on the bar chart to find out what sort of trouble you are having. Perhaps you have been using too few short, frequently used words.

If you press **F8** to obtain useful tips, the following appears:

```
Distance from focal point to ideal curve:
1 is good — 3 is too long

Spread of sentences on STYLE diagram:
8 is good — 4 is low

Compliance with ideal curve:
60% is good — 35% is low

Readability Index:
35 is good — 50 is too high

Percentage of mortar in text:
65% is good — 50% is too low

Percentage of sentences having only short words:
15% is good — 2% is low
```

What you can do to improve your writing

Too far from the ideal curve. – You have probably used too many long words and sentence structures that are too complicated. Simplify your writing!

Sentences spread is too narrow. – You need more word variation. Vary your sentence lengths and sentence structures more!

Poor compliance with ideal curve. – You have too few simple, narrative and elegant sentences and too few short, frequently used words in your text. Simplify your writing and use more mortar!

Readability Index is too high. – You have probably used too many long words relative to sentence lengths. Look at the style diagram. Use more short words or eliminate needlessly long words.

Too few sentences containing only short words. – Use more such sentences!

With a little practice, you'll be able to anticipate how the different displays are going to appear. Study the displays showing the results obtained from the analysis of Tom Sawyer.

General comments

Display 42 presents general comments on what you have done well in your text and also on what you can do to further improve readability.

Number of sentences and words

Display 43 tells you how many characters, words and sentences there are in your text. It also indicates how many long words and short words you have used in your text as well as the average number of short words per sentence and the average number of long words per sentence.

You can, for example, compare the length of your text with the number of times you have used certain bricks (display 22) to see how successful you have been in varying the words you choose.

How Readability was created

By Roland Larson

Style diagram – mathematical basis

This section will explain the mathematical analysis procedures on which the style diagram is based. To fully understand what is happening, you will need to know a lot about mathematics. But even if you have never studied math, you should be able to understand what happens in the different steps. Reading through the examples will give you a general idea of what the different formulas do.

Readability formulas

For some 50 years language researchers have been trying to measure the readability of different types of writing by means of mathematical formulas. In a book entitled **The Writing System** (1982), Edmond H. Weiss presents two readability formulas called the **Gunning Fog Index** and the **Recalculated Flesch Score**. Weiss believes that both formulas (the Gunning and the Flesch) survived for several decades because they were remarkably useful. They are more accurate and reliable than one would expect since they are so simple. They measure readability in a way that seems sensible to most people. The Fog Index formula has been modified as follows to obtain the Readabilty index used in your Readability program:

$$FOG = 0.4 * \left(\frac{\text{Number of words in text}}{\text{Number of sentences in text}} + 100 * \frac{\text{Number of hard words in text}}{\text{Number of words in text}} \right)$$

I have found that the definition that provides the best results is "hard words" = words longer than six letters. I have also discarded the 0.4 constant in the Fog Index formula since it affects only the value of the index. It does not affect the underlying principle.

$$R = \frac{\text{Number of words in text}}{\text{Number of sentences in text}} + 100 * \frac{\text{Number of long words in text}}{\text{Number of words in text}}$$

This Readability Index is 2.5 times as high as the original Fog Index.

A text consisting of five sentences containing a total of 110 words of which 25 are longer than six letters would thus have the following Readability Index.

$$R = \frac{110}{5} + 100 * \frac{25}{110} = 22 + 22.7 \approx 45$$

The higher the Readability Index, the more difficult the text is to read.

Here's how to interpret the different R values:

20–25 Very easy to read. Young people's books.

31–35 Easy to read. Novels and popular magazines.

40–45 Average. Normal newspaper articles.

50–55 Difficult. Normal value for government documents.

60– Very difficult. Bureaucratic gobbledygook.

The Readability formula indicates how a given text rates on a scale ranging from very easy to very difficult. For the reader, this index helps to explain why a text is difficult or easy to read. The writer, however, is interested in knowing how to improve the readability of his writing.

People frequently think that readability formulas indicate that one should write short sentences. It is easy to get this impression since "number of sentences in text" is part of the denominator, and this means that the more sentences the text contains the lower the index will be.

However, things are not quite that simple. If you look closer at the formula, you'll see that you can get the same index in a number of ways. A text consisting only of long sentences containing short words will obtain a high index. However, the same index can be obtained for a text that consists only of short sentences, but contains a relatively high percentage of long words.

A thorough mathematical analysis is needed to understand what the Readability formula and its counterparts actually provide. If you don't understand how the formula works, it will be difficult to draw the correct conclusions from the results it provides.

The following pages explain how readability formulas actually work. We will be working with the Readability Index formula on these pages, but if we had used some other readability formula, the same mathematical principles would apply.

To the best of our knowledge, no one has previously analyzed a readability formula in this way, even though they have been in existence for more than 50 years. The explanation you are about to read is thus the first of its kind.

Three variables become two

To make it somewhat easier to deal with the Readability formula mathematically, we shall use letters to designate the different variables.

$$R = \frac{\text{(number of words in text)}}{\text{(number of sentences in text)}} + 100 * \frac{\text{(number of long words in text)}}{\text{(number of words in text)}}$$

The above can be written as follows:

$$R = \frac{w}{s} + 100 * \frac{h}{w} \quad \dots\dots\dots\dots\dots\dots\dots\dots\dots\dots\dots\dots\dots \quad (1)$$

where R = Readability Index
      w = Number of words in text
      s = Number of sentences in text
      h = Number of long words in text

We shall now divide both the denominator and the numerator in the second term in (1) by s. This is permissible since:

$$\frac{s}{s} = 1$$

Formula (1) thus becomes

$$R = \frac{w}{s} + 100 * \frac{\dfrac{h}{s}}{\dfrac{w}{s}} \quad\text{...} \quad (2)$$

We can now simplify this formula so that it contains two variables:

$$R = x + 100 * \frac{y}{x} \quad\text{.....................................} \quad (3)$$

where R = Readability Index
x = w/s = Average number of words per sentence in text
y = h/s = Average number of long words per sentence in text

Since the Readability formula now contains only two independent variables, it can be represented on a coordinate system.

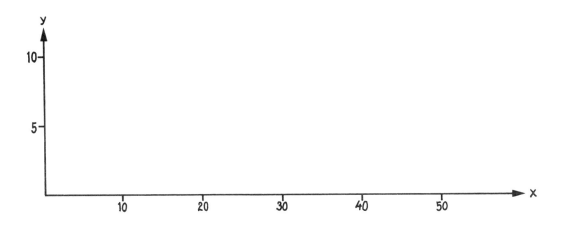

The lengths of the sentences are plotted along the x axis and the numbers of long words per sentence are plotted along the y axis.

Each text has a focal point

The average sentence length and the average number of long words per sentence can be plotted to find the focal point of a text.

In the example presented above, the focal point has the following coordinates: x = 22 and y = 5 due to the fact that:

$$x = \frac{110}{5} = 22 \quad \text{and} \quad y = \frac{25}{5} = 5$$

In the coordinate system the focal point is indicated by an asterisk.

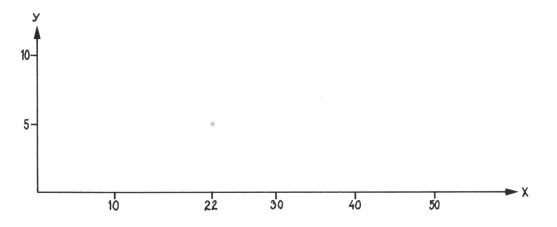

Focal point coordinates comprise Readability Index

From the above, we can see that it is easy to calculate the Readability Index (R) when we know the coordinates of the focal point. We simply use formula (3).

$$R = 22 + 100 * \frac{5}{22} = 22 + 22.7 = 44.7 \approx 45$$

Similarly, we can calculate the R for each focal point in our coordinate system. This may sound like a lot of work, but if we use a spreadsheet program it can be done quite easily. The results appear as follows. Each number indicates the Readability Index for a text that has its focal point at the point where the number appears in the coordinate system.

Long words per sentence	1	2	3	4	5	6	7	8	9	10	11	12	13	14	15	16	17	18	19	20	21	22	23	24	25	26	27	28	29	30
15															115	110	105	101	98	95	92	90	88	87	85	84	83	82	81	80
14														114	108	104	99	96	93	90	88	86	84	82	81	80	79	78	77	77
13													113	107	102	97	93	90	87	85	83	81	80	78	77	76	75	74	74	73
12												112	105	100	95	91	88	85	82	80	78	77	75	74	73	72	71	71	70	70
11											111	104	98	93	88	85	82	79	77	75	73	72	71	70	69	68	68	67	67	67
10										110	102	95	90	85	82	79	76	74	72	70	69	67	66	66	65	64	64	64	63	63
9									109	100	93	87	82	78	75	72	70	68	66	65	64	63	62	62	61	61	60	60	60	60
8								108	98	90	84	79	75	71	68	66	64	62	61	60	59	58	58	57	57	57	57	57	57	57
7							107	96	87	80	75	70	67	64	62	60	58	57	56	55	54	54	53	53	53	53	53	53	53	53
6						106	93	83	76	70	66	62	59	57	55	54	52	51	51	50	50	49	49	49	49	49	49	49	50	50
5					105	89	78	71	65	60	56	54	51	50	48	47	46	46	45	45	45	45	45	45	45	45	46	46	46	47
4				104	85	73	64	58	53	50	47	45	44	43	42	41	41	40	40	40	40	40	40	41	41	41	42	42	43	43
3			103	79	65	56	50	46	42	40	38	37	36	35	35	35	35	35	35	35	35	36	36	37	37	38	38	39	39	40
2		102	70	54	45	39	36	33	31	30	29	29	28	28	28	29	29	29	30	30	31	31	32	32	33	34	34	35	36	37
1	101	52	36	29	25	23	21	21	20	20	20	20	21	21	22	22	23	24	24	25	26	27	27	28	29	30	31	32	32	33
0	1	2	3	4	5	6	7	8	9	10	11	12	13	14	15	16	17	18	19	20	21	22	23	24	25	26	27	28	29	30
	1	2	3	4	5	6	7	8	9	10	11	12	13	14	15	16	17	18	19	20	21	22	23	24	25	26	27	28	29	30

Words per sentence

It thus becomes evident that a text's Readability Index is equal to the Readability Index at the focal point.

Let's check and see whether this holds true. Since the point defined by x = 22 and y = 5 provides a Readability Index of 45, it does.

Different focal points can have the same Readability Index (R)

Looking at the diagram, we see that there are a number of focal points that have Readability Indexes of 45:

a: x= 5, y= 2 provides R = 45   h: x=24, y= 5 provides R = 45
b: x=12, y= 4 provides R = 45   i: x=25, y= 5 provides R = 45
c: x=19, y= 5 provides R = 45   j: x=26, y= 5 provides R = 45
d: x=20, y= 5 provides R = 45   k: x=32, y= 4 provides R = 45
e: x=21, y= 5 provides R = 45   l: x=33, y= 4 provides R = 45
f: x=22, y= 5 provides R = 45   m: x=37, y= 3 provides R = 45
g: x=23, y= 5 provides R = 45   n: x=45, y= 0 provides R = 45

When we plot these 14 focal points on a coordinate system, we obtain the following:

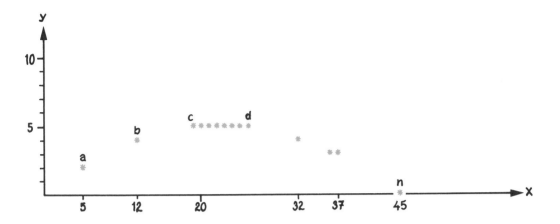

All of the texts which have their focal points at a, b, ... n thus have the same Readability Index, namely 45.

However, the text having its focal point at "a" is completely different from the text having its focal point at "n". The text with its focal point at "a" is written with very short sentences. Example:

"Writers must be good planners." has a sentence length of 5 words, 2 of which are long, and a Readability Index of 45.

The text with its focal point at "d" is wordy, since it consists of long sentences containing many short words. Example:

"You will be more successful in getting your point across if you use a simple writing style rather than words that have more obscure meanings." has a sentence length of 26 words, 5 of which are long, and a Readability Index of 45.

When you find that a text has a given Readability Index, it is thus difficult to know how it should be changed in order to improve readability. The texts at point "a" and at point "n" require entirely different remedial measures.

We have now seen that a Readability Index does not tell us very much unless we know where the text's focal point lies.

Readability Index parabolas

To find out and understand why a number of focal points have the same Readability Index, let's take a closer look at the Readability formula.

We shall start with formula (3):

$$R = x + 100 * \frac{y}{x}$$

We shall now determine the relationship between x and y for a fixed Readability Index designated R_1.

We now multiply all of the terms in (3) by x to obtain:

$$R_1 * x = x^2 + 100y$$

We shall now solve for y as a function of x.

$$y = \frac{R_1 x - x^2}{100} = \frac{x(R_1 - x)}{100} \dotfill (7)$$

Formula (7) defines a parabola, and all of the focal points that lie on this parabola will have the same Readability Index. Each such parabola (called a grade level parabola) passes through the origin and intersects the x axis a second time at a point that corresponds to Readability Index R_1.

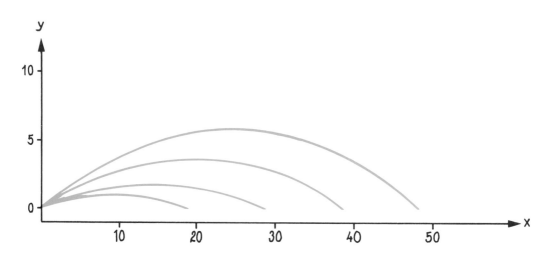

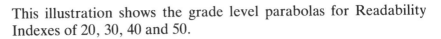

This illustration shows the grade level parabolas for Readability Indexes of 20, 30, 40 and 50.

Same focal point – different texts

Another important factor with which we should be familiar in order to evaluate a text is the extent to which sentences are spread (scattered) around the focal point.

If the sentences are grouped closely together, it indicates that the writer tends to use sentences having the same structure. He thus has a monotonous style.

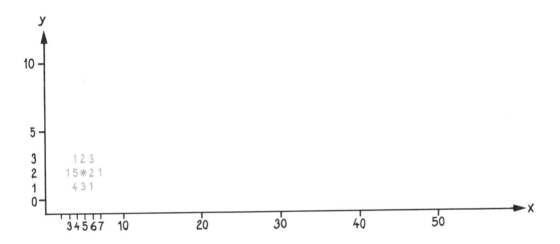

The numbers on the above diagram indicate how many sentences are located at the individual points. The text in the example thus contains $1 + 2 + 3 + 1 + 5 + 2 + 1 + 4 + 3 + 1 = 23$ sentences plus those (if any) that lie at the focal point itself.

It's much better if sentences are scattered throughout a large part of the diagram. This is usually the case for texts taken from novels. Look at the next diagram.

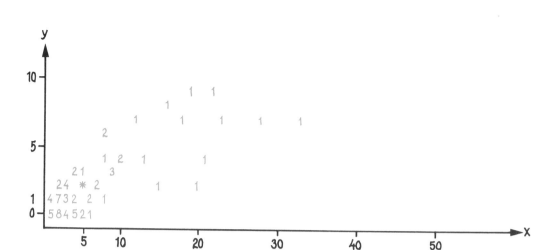

The two texts analyzed above have the same Readability Index (45) and the same focal point (5 words per sentence and 2 long words per sentence). But in spite of these similarities, they are very different.

The price of long words

A high Readability Index is the price we pay when we write too many long words. However, since long words convey valuable information, it is desirable to write as many long words as possible at the lowest possible "cost".

Let's take a closer look at how the Readability Index formula puts a price on long words.

We shall begin by looking at a Readability Index diagram.

Long words per sentence	1	2	3	4	5	6	7	8	9	10	11	12	13	14	15	16	17	18	19	20	21	22	23	24	25	26	27	28	29	30
15															115	110	105	101	98	95	92	90	88	87	85	84	83	82	81	80
14														114	108	104	99	96	93	90	88	86	84	82	81	80	79	78	77	77
13													113	107	102	97	93	90	87	85	83	81	80	78	77	76	75	74	74	73
12												112	105	100	95	91	88	85	82	80	78	77	75	74	73	72	71	71	70	70
11											111	104	98	93	88	85	82	79	77	75	73	72	71	70	69	68	68	67	67	67
10										110	102	95	90	85	82	79	76	74	72	70	69	67	66	66	65	64	64	64	63	63
9									109	100	93	87	82	78	75	72	70	68	66	65	64	63	62	62	61	61	60	60	60	60
8								108	98	90	84	79	75	71	68	66	64	62	61	60	59	58	58	57	57	57	57	57	57	57
7							107	96	87	80	75	70	67	64	62	60	58	57	56	55	54	54	53	53	53	53	53	53	53	53
6						106	93	83	76	70	66	62	59	57	55	54	52	51	51	50	50	49	49	49	49	49	49	49	50	50
5					105	89	78	71	65	60	56	54	51	50	48	47	46	46	45	45	45	45	45	45	46	46	46	47		
4				104	85	73	64	58	53	50	47	45	44	43	42	41	41	40	40	40	40	40	40	41	41	41	42	42	43	43
3			103	79	65	56	50	46	42	40	38	37	36	35	35	35	35	35	35	35	36	36	37	37	38	38	39	39	39	40
2		102	70	54	45	39	36	33	31	30	29	29	28	28	28	29	29	29	30	30	31	31	32	32	33	34	34	35	36	37
1	101	52	36	29	25	23	21	21	20	20	20	20	21	21	22	22	23	24	24	25	26	27	27	28	29	30	31	32	32	33
0	1	2	3	4	5	6	7	8	9	10	11	12	13	14	15	16	17	18	19	20	21	22	23	24	25	26	27	28	29	30
	1	2	3	4	5	6	7	8	9	10	11	12	13	14	15	16	17	18	19	20	21	22	23	24	25	26	27	28	29	30

Words per sentence

Let's assume that we wish to write a text having an average of 5 long words per sentence. What is the lowest Readability Index price that must be paid in order to do so? Line 5 in the above diagram tells us.

If we write five long words without any short words between them, the Readability Index will be 105. If we add one short word, thus increasing the sentence length to six words, the Readability Index drops to 89. By adding a second short word, we can reduce the Readability Index to 78, and by adding additional short words we can lower it to 71, 65, 60, 56, 54, 51, 50, 48, 47, 46, 46 and 45. We cannot lower it any further.

After we have added 14 short words and thus brought the length of the sentence to 19 words, we are down to a Readability Index of 45.

We cannot lower the Readability Index beneath 45. As you will note, the Readability Index does not rise even when we increase the number of short words added to 21. However, when we add the 22nd short word (thus bringing the sentence length to 27 words), the Readability Index starts to rise again.

It is thus evident that for each specific number of long words per sentence, there is a minimum Readability Index. And for each Readability Index, there is a maximum number of long words per sentence.

Maximum point on the grade level parabola

The lowest possible Readability Index for a given number of long words per sentence is at the maximum point on the grade level parabola.

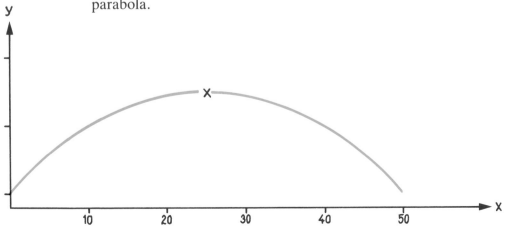

It's impossible to rise any higher on the y axis than the maximum point on the parabola, unless we are prepared to change to a higher parabola. The maximum point on a Readability Index parabola thus represents the ideal mixture of short and long words in sentences.

The coordinates of the maximum point can be found by differentiating formula (7).

$$y = \frac{R * x - x^2}{100}$$

(We changed from R_1 to R because we are now handling a general case.)

The derivative of y with regard to x is:

$$\frac{dy}{dx} = \frac{R - 2x}{100}$$

This means that the parabola reaches its maximum point when

$$x = \frac{R}{2} \quad \dots\dots\dots\dots\dots\dots\dots\dots\dots\dots\dots\dots\dots\dots\dots\dots\dots\dots\dots\dots\dots\dots \quad (8)$$

The second derivative is:

$$\frac{d_2\, y}{dx^2} = \frac{-2}{100}$$

Since the second derivative is negative, we have a maximum point.

Using (7), we can calculate the y coordinate of the maximum point:

$$y = \frac{x(R - x)}{100} = \frac{\frac{R}{2}(R - \frac{R}{2})}{100} = \frac{R^2}{400} \quad \dots\dots\dots\dots \quad (9)$$

Maximum point – ideal point

(8) and (9) show that the grade level parabolas have their maximum points at:

$$x = \frac{R}{2} \qquad\qquad y = \frac{R^2}{400}$$

The grade level parabola for a Readability Index of 45 thus passes through the origin and intersects the x axis at 45 and has its maximum point at:

$$x = \frac{45}{2} = 22.5 \approx 23 \qquad y = \frac{45^2}{400} = 5.0625 \approx 5$$

The maximum point of a Readability Index parabola is an ideal point. This is were the focal point should be on the diagram, since you cannot get a lower Readability Index for a given number of long words per sentence. Let's see where these maximum points lie for several Readability Indexes.

Since there is one maximum point for each Readability Index parabola and since there is one parabola for each Readability Index, there are an infinite number of ideal points. We shall now plot them on a curve.

Long words per sentence	1	2	3	4	5	6	7	8	9	10	11	12	13	14	15	16	17	18	19	20	21	22	23	24	25	26	27	28	29	30
15															115	110	105	101	98	95	92	90	88	87	85	84	83	82	81	80
14														114	108	104	99	96	93	90	88	86	84	82	81	80	79	78	77	77
13													113	107	102	97	93	90	87	85	83	81	80	78	77	76	75	74	74	73
12												112	105	100	95	91	88	85	82	80	78	77	75	74	73	72	71	71	70	70
11											111	104	98	93	88	85	82	79	77	75	73	72	71	70	69	68	68	67	67	67
10										110	102	95	90	85	82	79	76	74	72	70	69	67	66	66	65	64	64	64	63	63
9									109	100	93	87	82	78	75	72	70	68	66	65	64	63	62	62	61	61	60	60	60	60
8								108	98	90	84	79	75	71	68	66	64	62	61	60	59	58	58	57	57	57	57	57	57	57
7							107	96	87	80	75	70	67	64	62	60	58	57	56	55	54	54	53	53	53	53	53	53	53	53
6						106	93	83	76	70	66	62	59	57	55	54	52	51	51	50	50	49	49	49	49	49	49	49	50	50
5					105	89	78	71	65	60	56	54	51	50	48	47	46	46	45	45	45	45	45	45	45	45	46	46	46	47
4				104	85	73	64	58	53	50	47	45	44	43	42	41	41	40	40	40	40	40	40	41	41	41	42	42	43	43
3			103	79	65	56	50	46	42	40	38	37	36	35	35	35	35	35	35	35	35	36	36	37	37	38	38	39	39	40
2		102	70	54	45	39	36	33	31	30	29	29	28	28	28	29	29	29	30	30	31	31	32	32	33	34	34	35	36	37
1	101	52	36	29	25	23	21	21	20	20	20	20	21	21	22	22	23	24	24	25	26	27	27	28	29	30	31	32	32	33
0	1	2	3	4	5	6	7	8	9	10	11	12	13	14	15	16	17	18	19	20	21	22	23	24	25	26	27	28	29	30

Words per sentence

When plotted, the maximum points tend to create a parabola with its legs at the top and its minimum point at the origin. Let's find out whether this holds true.

Ideal curve

We shall now link all of the maximum points to form a coherent curve of ideal points. This can be done by finding the locations of the maximum points of the Readability Index parabolas. The curve thus obtained is called the ideal curve.

We shall start with (8) and (9).

$$x = \frac{R}{2} \quad \text{and} \quad y = \frac{R^2}{400}$$

Next, we shall try to find a mathematical expression that describes the relationships between x and y at the ideal points. And since we wish to do this for all of the Readability Indexes, we shall eliminate R from the above expression.

(8) and (9) can be rewritten as follows.

$R = 2x$ and $R^2 = 400y$

If we square the first expression, we obtain:

$R^2 = 4x^2$

We can now equate $400y$ with $4x^2$, since they are both equal to R^2.

$400y = 4x^2$

We have now obtained the relationship we were seeking:

$$y = \frac{x^2}{100} \quad \dotfill \quad (10)$$

Formula (10) is the ideal curve equation, and it can be plotted as follows:

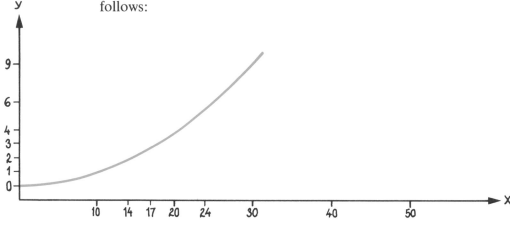

Human limitations

Some research has suggested that the human brain is forced to deal with more than nine concepts simultaneously, it groups them so that they will be easier to grasp. Thus to me, it's evident that we shouldn't ask the reader to deal with more than nine concepts in a single sentence. Moreover, if we insist on using 9 long words, we should write them in a sentence that has the lowest possible Readability Index.

What is the lowest Readability Index for a focal point that has nine long words? This question can be answered easily using formula (9):

$$R^2 = 400y$$

This provides the following expression for a Readability Index.

$$R = \sqrt{400} * y = 20\sqrt{y}$$

And when we give y a value of 9, we obtain:

$$R = 20 \sqrt{9} = 20 * 3 = 60$$

The Readability Index parabola for a Readability Index of 60 thus provides us with a warning curve that represents the outer limit beyond which no sentences should fall. Our diagram now appears as shown below:

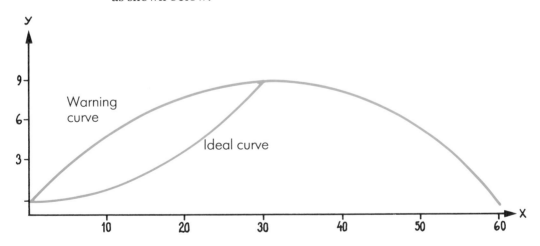

The above diagram can be interpreted as follows:

Try to write in such a way that the focal point of your text falls on, or at least close to, the ideal curve. However, this must not be interpreted to mean that each sentence has to lie on the ideal curve.

Quite the opposite, you should try to scatter (spread) your sentences to both the left and right of the ideal curve. Avoid writing sentences that fall above and to the left of the warning curve.

Proper balance around the ideal curve

As we see in the above illustration, the distance from the ideal curve to the left-hand part of the warning curve is shorter than the distance to the right-part of the warning curve. To obtain proper balance around the ideal curve, we should try to stay well to the left of the right-hand part of the warning curve.

We shall now derive an equation for the right-hand part of the limitation curve. The limitation curve encloses the ideal area, and the left-hand part of the limitation curve is congruent with the left-hand part of the warning curve.

First, we must obtain a mathematical expression for the distance from the ideal curve to the left-hand part of the warning curve. We shall call this distance D. Distance D varies, depending on how high along the y axis we measure. The expression we are seeking should thus be a function of y, $D = D(y)$.

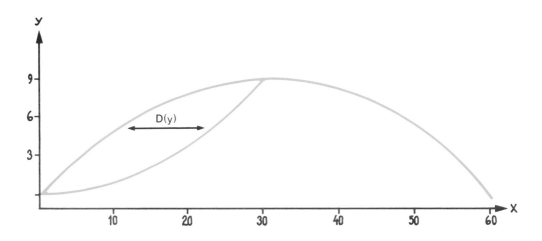

The distance in which we are interested is equal to the difference between the following two distances.

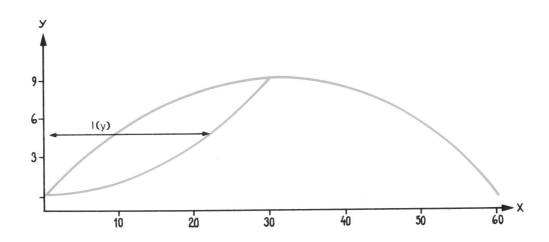

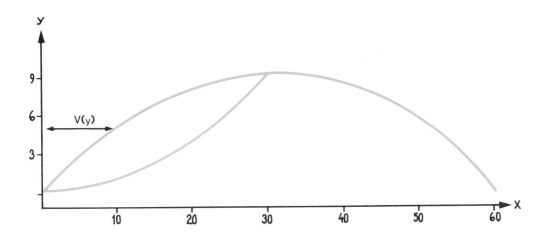

We now obtain the following equation:

$$D(y) = I(y) - V(y) \dots\dots\dots\dots\dots\dots\dots\dots\dots\dots\dots\dots\dots \ (11)$$

The right-hand part of the limitation curve is located to the right of the ideal curve and at the same distance, $D(y)$, from the ideal curve as the left-hand part of the warning curve.

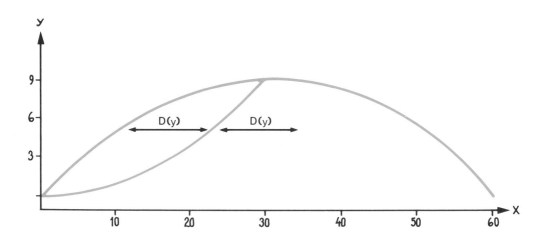

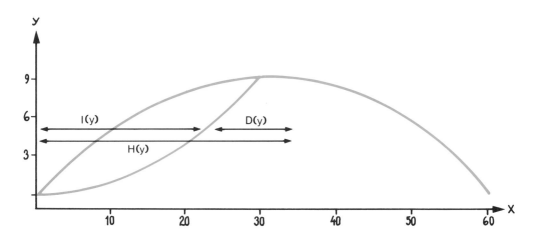

The distance from the y axis to the right-hand part of the limitation curve, H(y), is:

$$H(y) = I(y) + D(y)$$

If we now combine this with (11), we obtain the following:

$$H(y) = I(y) + D(y) = I(y) + I(y) - V(y) = 2I(y) - V(y) \ \dots\dots\dots \ (12)$$

Using (10), we can obtain an expression for I(y).

$$I(y) = x(y) = 10 \sqrt{y} \ \dots\dots\dots\dots\dots\dots\dots\dots\dots\dots\dots\dots\dots\dots\dots\dots \ (13)$$

V(y) is equal to what we obtain if we set L = 60 and solve the warning curve equation for x and this, in turn, is the same as what we would obtain by solving the Readability Index formula (3) for a Readability Index of 60. Using (3), we then obtain the following, which we can solve for x.

$$60x = x^2 + 100y$$

Since this is a second degree equation, we obtain two solutions, but we are only interested in one of them.

$$x_1 = 30 + \sqrt{900 - 100y} \ldots (14)$$

$$x_2 = 30 - \sqrt{900 - 100y} \ldots (15)$$

Since we are working with the left-hand part of the warning curve, we shall select solution (15) which provides us with the following for V(y).

$$V(y) = 30 - 10 \sqrt{9 - y} \quad\ldots\ldots\ldots\ldots\ldots\ldots\ldots\ldots\ldots\ldots\ldots\ldots (16)$$

Using (12), (13) and (16), we obtain:

$$H(y) = 20 \sqrt{y} - 30 + 10 \sqrt{9 - y} \quad\ldots\ldots\ldots\ldots\ldots\ldots\ldots\ldots\ldots (17)$$

For H(y), our diagram now appears as follows. We now have the teardrop shape into which good writing seems to fall. This provides strong support for the theories upon which my method is based.

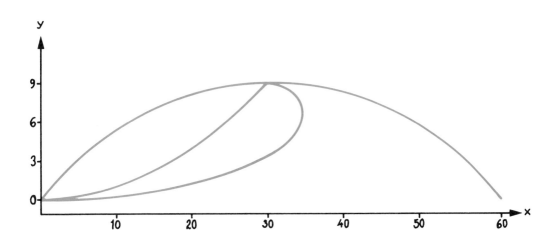

Conclusions

We have now derived the most important curves on the style diagram mathematically, and the diagram that we have obtained thus represents the mathematical results of the Readability Index formula that we started with. In this example, we started with the Gunning Fog Index Formula, but we could have obtained similar results using the Flesch, Coleman-Liau, or Kincaid formula.

When you analyze different texts with your Readability program, you will see that fiction (novels and the like) has a focal point that lies close to the ideal curve and, that at least 80–90 % of the sentences in fiction texts lie within the ideal area. Moreover, very few (if any) of the sentences in texts taken from fiction lie outside the left-hand part of the warning curve.

The Readability Index formula alone provides us only with average linguistic ratings. But by presenting the original data graphically in the form of a style diagram, we make it possible for a writer to ascertain which sentences in the text reduce readability.

Hopefully, this chapter has clarified to some extent the way that your Readability program works. Roland Larson, who created the program, will be pleased to receive comments. Address them to:

Roland Larson
Mandelblomsvägen 10
S-394 77 Kalmar SWEDEN

Appendix A. Error messages

DISK DRIVE NOT READY.
Cause: You forgot to insert a diskette in the drive or forgot to close the drive latch.
Action: Insert a diskette or close the latch.

PRINTER NOT READY.
Cause: You have not established proper contact with your printer. You may have forgotten to turn it on or forgotten to connect up the printer cable. Or perhaps the paper has run out.
Action: Check to see that the printer cable is connected (to the correct port). Check also to see that the printer is turned on and that it is properly loaded with paper.

SPECIFIED DIRECTORY NOT FOUND.
Cause: Incorrect subdirectory name or incorrect path.
Action: Enter the correct subdirectory name or correct path. Remember that you must start with a backslash. Example:

```
c:\word\texts
```

TEXT FILE NOT FOUND.
Cause: Wrong diskette, wrong subdirectory or wrong filename.
Action: Replace diskette or change to a new subdirectory. You can view the files that you have in any subdirectory by typing its name followed by a backslash. For example, you could type the following to see which files are contained in the subdirectory named Word on your hard disk:

```
c:\word\
```

Appendix B. Some useful DOS commands

This Appendix presents some useful DOS commands. Before you can use any of them, DOS must be ready to do your bidding. DOS indicates that it is ready by displaying the system prompt (A> or C>) on the screen.

The following commands are presented:

CD	Change subdirectory
COPY	Copy files
DEL	Delete files
DIR	Display list of filenames (directory)
DISKCOMP	Compare diskettes
DISKCOPY	Copy diskette
FORMAT	Format diskette
MD	Create subdirectory
RD	Delete subdirectory

Changing subdirectory (CD)

You can use this command when you wish to change to another subdirectory.

You can change to any desired subdirectory from any other subdirectory.

- Type:

  cd \   To reach the root subdirectory.

  Or:

  cd \spcsread   To change to the subdirectory that
                                          contains your Readability program, re-
                                          gardless of which subdirectory you are
                                          presently in.

  Or:

  cd \letter\quotes   To change to the QUOTES subdirec-
                                          tory which is found under LETTER
                                          which, in turn, is found under the root,
                                          regardless of which subdirectory you
                                          are presently in.

  Or:

  cd ..   To change to the subdirectory on the
                                          next higher level.

  Or:

  cd   To see which subdirectory you are pre-
                                          sently in.

- Press the ↵ key.

When the system prompt appears again, the subdirectory will have been changed.
Subdirectory names must comply with the same rules as filenames, but they can
only consist of up to eight characters (no extension permitted).

You can also see which subdirectory you are in by executing the DIR command.

- Type:

  dir *.

- Press the ↵ key.

The following will now appear on the screen, thus indicating which subdirectory you are in.

```
Volume in drive A has no label

 Directory of C:\LETTER\QUOTES
```

You can copy to and from a subdirectory by specifying a path. This is described in greater detail in the DOS manual that accompanies your computer.

Copying individual files (COPY)

The COPY command is used to copy individual files.

- Insert the source diskette containing the files that are to be copied into diskette drive A.

- Insert the target diskette onto which the files are to be copied into diskette drive B.

- Type:

copy a:*.* b:/v

This copies all files from diskette drive A to diskette drive B, and the copying is verified.

Or:

copy a:*.rdb b:/v

This copies all files with name extensions of in RDB from diskette drive A to diskette drive B, and the copying is verified.

Or:

copy a:test.rdb b:/v

This copies the file named TEST.RDB from diskette drive A to diskette drive B and the copying is verified.

Or:

copy c:\test*.* a:/v

This copies all files in the TEST subdirectory on hard disk C to the diskette in drive A and the copying is verified.

Or:

```
copy c:\test\*.* c:\tlf /v
```

This copies all files in the TEST sub-directory on hard disk C to subdirectory TLF on hard disk C, and the copying is verified.

Or:

```
copy a:test.rdb prn
```

This copies the file named TEST.RDB to the printer, i.e. you obtain a single hard copy of the file (don't forget to make certain that the printer is ON LINE before starting).

- Press the ⏎ key.

When the system prompt appears, copying is completed:

```
      1 File(s) copied

A>_
```

Deleting files (DEL)

To delete files, you can use the DEL command as follows:

- Insert the diskette containing the files you wish to delete into diskette drive A.
- Type:

```
del a:*.*
```

This deletes all files from diskette drive A.

Or:

```
del b:*.*
```

This deletes all files from diskette drive B.

Or:

```
del a:*.rdb
```

This deletes all files with name extensions of RDB from diskette drive A.

Or:

del a:test.rdb   This deletes the TEST.RDB file from
                                        diskette drive A.

- Press the ↵ key.

When the system prompt appears again on the screen, deletion is completed.

Displaying a directory (DIR)

When you wish to display the directory containing the names of all the files on a
diskette, you can use the DIR command as follows:

- Insert the diskette in drive A.
- Type:

dir   This displays all filenames on the dis-
                                        kette in the default drive.

Or:

dir b: This displays all filenames in drive B.

Or:

dir *.rdb   This displays all filenames extended
                                        with RDB.

Or:

dir c:\test*.rdb   This displays all filenames extended
                                        with RDB in the TEST subdirectory
                                        on hard disk C.

Or:

dir /p   This displays all filenames, 23 at a
                                        time.

Or:

dir /w   This displays all filenames in five col-
                                        umns.

- Press the ↵ key.

Comparing two diskettes (DISKCOMP)

You can compare the contents of two diskettes after you have copied them (but only if you have used DISKCOPY).

• Insert the DOS diskette in diskette drive A.

• Type:

```
diskcomp a: b:
```

• Press the ↵ key.

The following will appear on the screen:

```
Insert first diskette in drive A:
Insert second diskette in drive B:
Strike any key when ready
```

• Insert the original diskette in diskette drive A.

• Insert the diskette containing the copy (which is to be compared with the content of the original diskette) in diskette drive B.

• Press the ↵ key.

When the following appears on the screen, the comparison has shown that the contents of the diskettes are identical:

```
Diskette compare ok
Compare more diskettes (Y/N)?
```

• Press the **N** key if you wish to conclude comparison. Press the **Y** key if you wish to compare other diskettes.

Copying an entire diskette (DISKCOPY)

You can copy the entire content of a diskette onto another diskette by means of DISKCOPY. The diskette onto which you are copying need not be formatted, since this is done automatically by DISKCOPY.

• Insert the DOS diskette in diskette drive A.

- Type:

  ```
  diskcopy a: b:
  ```

- Press the ← key.

The following will appear on your screen:

```
Insert source diskette in drive A:
Insert target diskette in drive B:
Strike any key when ready
```

- Insert the diskette containing whatever you wish to copy into diskette drive A.
- Insert the diskette onto which you wish to copy into diskette drive B.
- Press the ← key.

When the following appears on your screen, copying has been completed:

```
Copy another (Y/N)?
```

- Press the **N** key if you wish to conclude copying. Press the **Y** key if you wish to copy another diskette.

Formatting a diskette (FORMAT)

When you wish to prepare (format) a diskette for use, proceed as follows:

- Insert the DOS diskette into diskette drive A.
- Type:

  ```
  format b:
  ```
  If you wish to format a text file diskette.

  Or:

  ```
  format b:/s
  ```
  If you wish to format a program diskette that you can use to boot (start) your system.

- Press the ← key.

The following will appear on your screen:

```
Insert new diskette for drive B:
and strike any key when ready
```

- Insert the diskette that is to be formatted into diskette drive B.
- Press the ↵ key.

When the following appears on your screen, formatting has been completed:

```
Format another (Y/N)?
```

- Press the **N** key if you wish to conclude formatting. Press the **Y** key if you wish to format another diskette.

Creating a subdirectory (MD)

When you create a subdirectory, you must remember that you can only create a subdirectory located one step down in the tree. This means that you must first change to the subdirectory that is to be one level above the one that you are going to create.

You must first change to the subdirectory from which you wish to create the new one. For example, if you wish to have a subdirectory located immediately beneath the root, you must change to the root as follows:

- Type:

  cd\

- Press the ↵ key.

The root directory is now the default (active) directory. That is to say, it is the one that will be shown when you type DIR. And when you create a new subdirectory, it will be linked to the root.

- Type:

  md test

- Press the ↵ key.

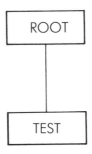

When the system prompt appears on the screen again, you will have created a subdirectory called TEST. The name of a subdirectory must comply with the same rules as those set forth for filenames, although it can only consist of up to eight characters (no extension permitted).

You can check to see that the subdirectory was created by issuing the DIR command:

* Type:

   `dir *.`

* Press the ⏎ key.

You will see on the screen that a subdirectory called TEST has been created.

```
TEST   <DIR>    1-23-1987    12:24a
```

If you wish to change to another subdirectory, see the section headed Changing subdirectory (CD).

Deleting a subdirectory (RD)

This command can be used when you wish to delete a subdirectory.

Two conditions must be fulfilled before you can delete a subdirectory, namely:

* The subdirectory must be empty, i.e. it must not contain any files or other subdirectories.

- You must be in the subdirectory on the next higher level or the root directory if it is on the next higher level.

- Type:

  `rd test`

- Press the ↵ key.

You have now deleted the subdirectory named TEST.

Appendix C. Customizing Readability

When starting Readability you can specify directly the drive where the glossary can be found, where the texts for analysis are likely to be located, and where analysis results should be stored. You can specify the name of the glossary you want the program to use; and if you're using a hard disk, you can specify subdirectories and paths.

To specify a glossary's drive, path and name, write the information in the following form.

- Type:

  ```
  read l=c:\spcsread\synlist.nr2
  ```

To specify the first place the program should look for files to be analyzed, you can use the same format with the letter T being used.

- Type:

  ```
  read t=c:\spcsword
  ```

To specify where results should be stored, use the same format, but with the letter R being used.

- Type:

  ```
  read r=b:
  ```

Especially if you've got a hard disk, you may want to use your word processor to modify the file READ.BAT, which is created in the C: root directory when you use the HDCOPY.BAT program to install Readability on a hard disk. Normally, all READ.BAT contains is the following:

```
CD \SPCSREAD
READ
CD
```

To instruct the program to always look in your word processing subdirectory (named \SPCSWORD) for a special glossary named LAWYER.LTK, to look for files to analyze in the same subdirectory, and to store the analysis results in another directory named \FINAL, just modify READ.BAT to read as follows:

```
CD \SPCSREAD
READ L=C:\SPCSWORD\LAWYER.LTK  T=C:\SPCSWORD  R=C:\FINAL
CD \
```

By changing the READ.BAT file in this way, you can save a few minutes every time you start to use Readability. And, with the instructions we've gone over in this chapter thus far, you can also change these options anytime they don't apply.

Index

Program license agreement

READ THIS AGREEMENT CAREFULLY!

Scandinavian PC Systems AB produces high-quality programs and sells them at very low prices. Our business idea is to market programs and manuals in volumes high enough to justify our low price.

We thus respectfully request that you observe the following:

1. You may:

    a. Use this program on a single computer.

    b. Make copies of this program for your own use.

    c. Transfer this program to a third party who accepts these conditions. If you transfer the program, you must transfer all copies to the same third party. Any that are not transferred must be destroyed.

2. You must not:

    a. Use this program on more than one computer. By way of example, an instructor must purchase a separate program for each computer used by his students or trainees.

    b. Disassemble or decompile the program.

    c. Export the program without the written permission of *Scandinavian PC Systems AB*.

Warranty

Scandinavian PC Systems AB herewith warrants that on delivery your diskette is free of material faults and processing errors. Beyond this, *Scandinavian PC Systems AB* does not provide any type of warranty regarding the program's characteristics and does not warrant that it will be suitable for your applications. Neither does *Scandinavian PC Systems AB* assume any responsibility whatsoever for any damages that may occur in connection with the use of the program.